MW01234358

DRAFT

Thank you sir
for your support

CRITICAL SUCCESS

The 2 Rules of 3

D. S. BROWN

authorHOUSE®

AuthorHouse™
1663 Liberty Drive, Suite 200
Bloomington, IN 47403
www.authorhouse.com
Phone: 1-800-839-8640

First published by AuthorHouse 1/30/2008

ISBN: 978-1-4343-5504-1 (sc)

Printed in the United States of America
Bloomington, Indiana

This book is printed on acid-free paper.

This book is dedicated to my Dads,

The one who created me,

John Heard Brown

And the one who supported me,

Michael Forsythe Lindsey

I will always love you

TABLE OF CONTENTS

INTRODUCTION

Let's face it. We all want to be rich.

Do you like the way it sounds as it rolls off the tongue? *I want to be rich!* As it is said, you feel the implicit promise of a guaranteed tomorrow. You can just see it now. When, when, when. When you make your first million, you're going to buy a house for your mother. You're going to live in a mansion and have a vacation home on the Caribbean coast. You'll own a Ferrari. Actually you'll be so rich you'll have your own G4, a private plane to whisk you off to parts unknown to lesser mortals. Or, even better, the G4 might fly you to your own Caribbean island. Forget a beach house. You own your very own coastline. It surrounds your personal paradise estate, complete with an airstrip. Yes, you have plans. It's simply a matter of when it will all happen.

Some people like to fantasize about this fabulous tomorrow and can't wait to buy the next lottery ticket. They just know they're going to hit the winning number. Their number is destined to come up. They're feeling particularly lucky.

Some people know they need a plan, and for the past few years they've attended seminar after seminar. They've joined multiple multi-level marketing corporations. They keep going because they know the truth; that one of these seminars will teach them how to become a real estate lord or master stock manipulator, or the inventor of the world's most innovative product since the light bulb.

Something is going to happen, and one of these people will become the luckiest person in the world. From this, they will have the ability to purchase all the material wants their hearts desire. They will floss. They will flash. They will bling, bling to their heart's content. Oh, what a wonderful something they will be when they become rich.

Yes, this is how we think. This is how we are conditioned to think. It is ingrained in us culturally. Through the power of Media-Driven ConsumerCelebreality, we have become mindless Myrmidons, following famed Achilles to an absurd death, an arrow through the ankle.

The blame is twofold. The drive for more profit is the American way, the entrepreneurial way. It is a good way, so long as it is tempered with justice, morality, and common sense. This is not always the case.

However, in truth, the lion's share of the blame belongs to the individual, to you and me. What's the problem? Can we not think? Granted, we all think, to some degree. Unfortunately we don't think critically. We don't consider. We don't question. We're Myrmidons. We're spoons.

We have to learn to be strong individuals in order to better the whole. We have to be good to ourselves in order to be good to others. We have to discover our true passion and work to achieve it. We need to understand what being rich truly means. What does it mean for the family, for the individual, for you, for me? Do you truly understand wealth? Do you know what *rich* means? And what about justice? How does justice come into play when a group of people—call them shareholders—want to make money legitimately, honestly, above board, but not necessarily morally?

Too much morality, just like too much religion, can cause way too much trouble. Just like anything, you need enough to be just, to be right. It's all-good in moderation. Sometimes, given a situation, it's better to be more moral than most. If you were a worker at Enron, when it was America's so-called greatest company, and you were privy to what was going on, you might have become a whistleblower and alerted the authorities, or at the very least quit the company. This is how you should be moral, standing against criminal activity. However, sometimes, for the good of the individual as well as the whole, it's good to skirt the edge, to be less moral than most. Sometimes you might have to offend someone just to get a point across in order to achieve understanding and morality for everyone as opposed to just one group. For more insight into how morally absurd we can become, watch a program called *Moral Oral*. Some of you will be offended. Some of you will understand. It's important that you do comprehend how morality impacts your wealth. In regard to your habits, it's a factor that culturally holds sway over you, me—all of us.

Let me be honest with you. The person I described above, the person that attended seminars and saw riches just around the corner, was me. If you see yourself in these words, don't feel bad. We're only human, and we most certainly make mistakes. History has shown us that we're darn good followers. If we find a message that resonates with us, makes us feel strong and passionate, then we'll latch on to it with everything we have, whether it's fascism or bling-bling. We're rabid followers. This is you. This is me. We must become stronger individuals, priding ourselves on individual thought and independent action. We must become critical thinkers.

As a person trying to become a critical thinker, I find myself thinking about the nature of being rich. I find myself considering wealth. I notice that when I think about justice, I'm moved to think about what the word truly means to me, how I perceive it in regard to the world around me, and how it relates to wealth, equity, and opportunity. I find myself wanting to be successful, given the opportunities that should be afforded to everyone. I understand that this success I crave is critical to my wellbeing. I take it seriously. So should you.

So, what is *rich*?

Being rich is simply defined as having wealth or great possessions, abundantly supplied with resources, means, or money. It can also mean having valuable resources, as in "a rich country." It also means costly, expensively elegant, or fine. It can also mean sumptuous or elaborately abundant, like a rich feast or a rich gravy, or dark chocolate cake.

And what is wealth?

Wealth is an abundance or profusion of anything, plenty, a great quantity, valuable contents or product, and of course, that state of being rich. Warren Buffett is a very wealthy man.

And let us state how Dictionary.com defines *justice*. Oh, and for those of you who don't know me, you'll find that I'm a strong advocate of reading and expanding your vocabulary. So I don't want to get any emails about my using "big words." Only ignorant people say such things. Go get a dictionary and look up any word you don't understand. This too is an exercise in becoming a critical thinker. Now back to defining justice.

Justice is the quality of being just, righteousness, equitableness, or moral rightness. It is also the moral principle of determining just conduct. It is also conformity to this just conduct, as manifested by just conduct, dealing, or treatment. Lastly it is administering deserved punishment or reward.

When most of you think about justice you thank about the last definition. You think about what is righteous and how a criminal must be punished for his or her misdeeds. It's the common definition that we're all familiar with, and it is the one that most often may come to mind. However, it is just conduct that concerns us in this context. We all want and demand equal treatment. We all want a fair handshake.

Now, how do all these tie together? When I think about it, what conclusion can I draw from these words that's of critical importance to me and my success? I'll start with justice. I expect opportunity. I demand the chance to prove myself, to realize my full potential. Despite my ethnicity and the lingering affects of a wayward nation's primitive social sensibilities, I know my home is the best place in the world for me to attempt to achieve my own critical success. If I do not receive justice in my fair and lawful pursuit of success, I have legal recourse. I can use the rule of law to bring justice to my transgressor. I understand, from a rational standpoint, that I want justice and that for all intents and purposes, until a given situation proves otherwise, I have it.

Some of us consider what corporate America is doing unjust. Some consider the affects of media-driven consumercelebreality to be downright criminal. I'm inclined to agree. The efforts of mighty corporations have turned our nation away from saving and moved us toward continuous spending and the irrationality of thinking of your home as an ATM, which one may use to buy more and more stuff. Unfortunately, the truth is those of us who think along these lines are responding with critical emotions as opposed to critical cognition. The mighty corporate machine is nothing more than some people working fervently at the behest of a host of shareholders (more people, some of them quite bright) to realize their own success, which capitalism and free enterprise readily support. If we seek to limit their right to make money, we limit ourselves. In truth we must step back, stop, and think! While we demand they behave responsibly, we must force ourselves to maintain personal accountability. As adults we must teach our youth, be the example, demand that the corporations step peddling so much junk, and at the same time stop buying it. If you don't need it, don't wonder into the mall and buy it. Don't be a hypocrite. Don't be a spoon.

Have I thought critically about my wealth? Yes, I have. As of late I have been considering it more and more. I am very, very wealthy. I don't have a great deal of money. However, I am working to change that. I understand that my personal wealth isn't about my bank account. And it is certainly not about my material possessions. I am wealthy in friendship, at home, and at work. I am wealthy in family, even though some family members leave a lot to be desired. I love them nonetheless, and they enrich my life greatly. I am wealthy in mind and body. I am able-bodied. I can earn a living. I am wealthy in spirit. I have faith.

What truly makes me wealthy?

I'll tell you. I already mentioned my mind. However, how I use it provides me with my greatest wealth. I am attempting to grow in critical thinking skills. By doing this I am learning to slow down from the rapid pace of manic America. I am learning to consider. I am learning to understand and rationalize. I am relearning how to think.

How does this make me wealthy? People, by thinking, I can divine my way from one state of wealth to another. One state of wealth is personal security, family and friends, a roof over my head, more food in my refrigerator than the majority of the people on planet Earth, a steady job, and a life in which my weekends can be spent lying by a lake, doing absolutely NOTHING! That's wealthy, people! I will use my mind to add to my already expansive wealth. I will move to a second state of wealth—one where my bank account affords me the opportunity to fly to Rome on a whim, to spend a weekend shopping in New York, or take my family on holiday in the South Pacific.

I have already started doing this. I encourage you to do the same. How, you ask? I started moving to this second state of wealth by reducing my overall debt. Then I started working on increasing my income. I worked hard to earn a promotion at work. At the same time, I worked on divining the *second rule of critical success*. I was woefully unsuccessful, but the experience provided me with knowledge. It was a working education, and it clearly defined the principles I would come to espouse around personal financial growth. The effort proved to be successful in educating me, despite the steep financial cost. I'll share more of this experience with you later.

So, am I rich? Hell yes! And at this moment, right now, as I type (in the past for you), I have less than three thousand dollars in the bank. And my wonderful banking institution has somehow managed to misplace $2,500 of my hard-earned income. I have taken a deep breath, and I'm waiting for their offices to open. No sweat, I'm still rich. I've explained to you my state of wealth.

I'm steadily building on this wealth. I have one more credit card to pay off, and I will be credit-debt-free. Now, some of the people I like to listen to, like Clark Howard and Suze Orman, may tell you that you should be saving, or paying yourself, while you kill off your credit debt.

They're right!

I say again: they're right. People, you need to start saving, building your wealth, as soon as possible. However, as with any equation, there are permutations. I know they're correct, I just decided to do it differently. This was a personal decision. My wife and I are expecting a child. I did not want to bring her into this world with a mountain of credit card debt. We took one year, cut expenses, paid off our vehicles, refinanced our house, and threw everything we had at our debt. It was dangerous. We were hit with new expenses. However, we managed them. In the end, we achieved our objective. We were credit-debt-free. We sleep worry-free and plan for our future wealth with multiple investments, college savings plans, tight budgets, and entrepreneurial visions.

My friends, I am rich in family. I am rich in thought. I am rich in action. I am rich in planning. I am rich. Through critical thinking, I will achieve critical success. I will only grow richer. So please, I urge you to join me on this journey. Take the time to understand the information I relay to you. Allow me to share with you all that I have learned. And, together, let us work toward achieving what everyone is entitled to: CRITICAL SUCCESS!

CHAPTER 1
WHAT IS CRITICAL SUCCESS?

What is critical success?

KA-CHOW POW WOW!

I'M GONNA SHOW HOW TO MAKE GOO-GOBS OF MONEY!

I'M TALKIN' ABOUT MONEY FLOWIN' OUT THE BACK OF YOUR BUTT! WE'RE TALKING COLD, HARD CASH!

DOLLARS, MY FRIEND!

ME!

YOU!

TOGETHER!

YOU'LL EARN $10,000 IN A WEEK.

YOU'LL BE MAKING TWO MILLION DOLLARS A YEAR!

All you need to do is pick up my free CD. I'll tell you all about my program and why it will revolutionize your life.

Pick up the CD!

IT'S FREE!

Poor poetry, my friends, definitely poor poetry.

After you pick up the CD and listen to the tantalizing details, you learn that for three easy payments of $39.95, you will get all the detailed information you need in order to realize success. You smile. You're so excited on the inside that you begin to fairly glow on the outside. In fact, you're shining like the sun. And people see it. It's amazing.

Let's break it down. For three easy payments of $39.95, totaling $119.85 (not including shipping), you get a nice DVD packed full of advertising and more tantalizing facts. You get a manual that tells you how to buy real estate, where to look, and what kind of tricks you can use to close the deal and make money at the closing table. You get free pointers. You get a guide to training courses that will be offered in your area for only $99.95. For fifty cents a minute, you can call the staffed help line, and someone will guide you through those difficult deals. Okay, sounds good.

But wait, there's more!

For an additional $59.95, you can get the step-by-step Hot Money From Foreclosures Quick-Flip Program Manual and DVD, specifically designed for those aggressive real estate entrepreneurs that want to venture into the incredibly lucrative field of flipping foreclosures. Call and order TODAY!

Wow.

I mean, really, I almost want to buy the program myself. It sounds so damn hot I can't help myself. Well, to be honest, I bought one of these programs before. I copied the material and sent it back, so I only wound up paying for shipping. I didn't want the CDs (no DVDs back then). I figured I could get it all from reading. I'm pretty big on reading.

Know what I found?

In my area the no money-down methods the manual outlined were not being utilized. Financial instruments like assumable mortgages were not in common use. And making a deal with a desperate homeowner about to be out on the street is a lot harder than it seems.

Now here's where it gets interesting. I used the check-sheets that were provided. I structured loans on my property targets. I pulled the trigger. The program actually worked. However, what was disconcerting was the fact that I later found all this information for free on the Internet. I even went to Barnes & Noble and found it in some Real Estate books for considerably less. Still, I had my property. I can't say I didn't learn something from the program. What bothers me is that, if I had been thinking about it, I could have done my own investigation and avoided the time and expense altogether. However, I have to say the experience was worthwhile.

You can learn something from just about anything. Understand, I got lucky. I was trying to become a critical thinker, even back then.

Some friends I know went the same route. They bought the program. They attended the seminar. They went on learning trips. They went to more seminars. They purchased training programs. They spent a great deal of money. They tried to flip a house. They went into steep debt. The whole experiment was a failure. The program didn't spend enough time teaching them about the risks of what they were attempting to do. They didn't see the pitfalls. They didn't gauge the local real estate market. They weren't into the details, checking their figures to try and preserve their profit going into the deal, well before signing at the closing table. All of these failures cost them dearly. All of their program materials are gathering dust in a corner. One of my friends recently attended a day-trading seminar. He's moving on to the next thing, confident in the fact that he will get rich quickly.

The truth? I fell for this one too, back in 1999 and 2000. However, I got my education the hard way and didn't give some pie-faced clown my money just so he could teach me how to look at a screen and wait for it to turn green, so I could blow my hard-earned cash on a hot stock, jumping into it at the top end of a momentum swing. He's getting rich off of the money he receives for selling his program, and the idiotic blinking red-and-green buy/sell software. The man probably doesn't even own large positions in any one stock—at least not since he learned he could make a lot more money with his intellectual property and a nifty infomercial.

None of the getting-rich programs will lead you to critical success. Why? Because they purport to show how easy it is to make money and get rich. They say they can guide you to the Promised Land; just follow their lead. They tell you to think, but just so much. After all, why do you have to do the heavy lifting? They have it all laid out for you on page after page of scintillating material, purportedly just as good as an option on a guaranteed delivery bar of gold.

Some people will achieve success through these programs. It won't be you. Invariably you will be the person watching the video of the person who made $27,000 on a real estate deal at the closing table, or that other kid who looks like a space cadet yet made $18,000 on one stock option deal. You want to be that person. Yet you don't have the true fire and passion to become that person the hard way. You buy into the allure of the program—the quick fix, the get-rich-quick scheme—all the while making the owners of the program that much richer.

I'm going to be honest with you. My program is no different than theirs from the pure standpoint of free-enterprise and entrepreneurialism. I want you to use my program. I want you to purchase my intellectual material. I want to make money through my efforts. I have found I have a passion for the written word, and at this moment in my life I enjoy writing motivational material. This book in particular details my thoughts on how to be successful, and I want to share it with you, for a fee. I have no desire to abuse you. I simply want to help, and reap some reward for my efforts. However, I don't want to lead you astray. I want to re-socialize you. I want you to embrace critical thinking. I want you to appreciate hard work. I want you learn patience. I want you to achieve success. And I want you to understand how to appreciate it. The best way to do this is to truly earn it through diligence and hard work. For this reason I have written this book.

So again we arrive at the question, what is critical success? Let's break it down into its constituent components:

What is Critical?	Involving skillful judgment as to truth and merit. Pertaining to or of the nature of a crisis. Of decisive importance with respect to the outcome, urgent, and essential.
What is Success?	The favorable or prosperous termination of attempts or endeavors. The attainment of wealth, position, or honors. The achievement of something planned, intended, or desired.

So, let's ask the question one more time: what is critical success?

CRITICAL SUCCESS is the planned achievement of something urgent and essential, utilizing skillful planning and judgment for the express purpose of attaining personal prosperity.

My friends, we are not utilizing skillful planning and judgment when we spend our hard-earned dollars on get-rich-quick schemes, putting all our hopes and dreams into someone else's plan for building wealth. That's not critical thinking.

I am a fan of Clark Howard's advice. I listen to his show several days out of the week. I have Eric Edelman's book on my shelf at work. I listen to Suze Orman. However, with all their knowledge and skill, I do not take what they have to offer on face value alone. No, I listen. I question. I evaluate, and I incorporate. I have made some of their ideas my own. It is how I moved into a state of wealth that was credit-debt-free. I continue to listen to them, adjusting my plans for the future. I also look at other sources of information, sifting and discerning. I question. I plan. I make every attempt to digest information critically, incorporating some ideas and discarding others.

All my life I have wanted to be successful. However, unfortunately for me, I always had my eye set firmly on the end prize, the objective. I never spent enough time thinking about how I was going to get there. I eventually found myself thinking about the process of building wealth. Actually the wealth was secondary. I kept concentrating on different ideas, different businesses, inventions, things of this sort. I thought about how I might go about realizing my dreams, but I still wasn't thinking critically. I tried real estate. I tried the stock market. I tried entrepreneurship. However, never did I think critically about what I was doing. I never had a good plan. Can you remember the old saying?

Those who fail to plan, plan to fail.

It is so very true. I attacked all my ideas with zeal. I was ambitious. I was quick. I thought things through, or so I thought. I had a positive attitude. I was confident. Still, I wasn't critical. My tiny little foray into real estate proved to be successful, after my dealings with crack-dealing tenants and thieves. I was able to sell my property for a substantial profit, which I had to use to pay off my accumulated debt from the stock market. I had a plan, and it was called *a mess*.

You have to be careful about making a mess. Mess can cost you money. It certainly cost me some money. I had planned, but I had not planned skillfully, utilizing sound judgment. Even if I had used sound judgment, I probably still would have failed. The dot-com era was devastating to many. However, I took my errors and promptly messed up two or three more times. I still attended some seminars. I still held out some hope. It took me awhile to understand the truth. I had to slow down, discuss the issue with some like-minded friends, and finally learn and apply critical thinking skills.

I had to stop and think.

The first thing I realized was that throughout all my manic plan-less planning, over time I had become a whale of debt. I distinctly remember spending thousands of dollars, foolishly believing that my profits from the stock market would cover all the debt I was creating. WRONG!

Yes, I had to slow down—slow, slower, and finally stop. I had to stop and think! It was critically important to do so. I stopped, looked around, took stock of my situation, and I rapidly realized I was heading nowhere fast. Trying to get rich quick, and having an insanely spoonish desire to look wealthier than I really was, was the SINGLE MOST CRITICAL THING KEEPING ME FROM MY GOAL OF ATTAINING WEALTH.

I had to capitalize that sentence because I want you to understand just how important this single point is. It affects all of us. Our wants and our desires have become the most important things in our lives. They are really voracious beasts that devour us from inside, fed by the media-driven consumercelebreality industrial complex, ever ready to indulge the masses. Everything from your need for empty calories in cereal to your insane desire for ridiculously overvalued diamonds is fed to you through the media. We're spoons on sheep's feet, being led to financial slaughter—all because we simply don't think.

We're being raised to think that life takes Visa. NO, IT DOES NOT! Visa should be a tool for you to use responsibly, not a facilitator for your personal and familial wellbeing. Your life does not require CREDIT, no matter how many commercials convince you otherwise. You should dismiss this as an outright lie, because it is! As critical thinking beings, we have to reeducate ourselves on our true wants and needs. A $75,000 car is not something you need, even if your $12,000 car is not providing you enough legroom. We are being raised to try to keep up with the Joneses, the Smiths, the Robinsons, the Wangs, and the Cortezes. We need to concentrate more on keeping up with our own finances and growing wealth, instead of worrying about what type of luxury vehicle Amy Wang is driving this year.

However, I do acquiesce. The lure of our complex media-driven consumercelebreality culture is powerful. I've been caught up in it. I spent years chasing dreams on a wing and a prayer. The dreams weren't bad ones. It was simply the only way I knew how to think at the time. I didn't concentrate on process and planning. I didn't use the secret and thereby allow myself to uncover the specific processes required and objectives necessary to reach my ultimate goal of critical success. I've since matured. And I would like to share that story with you.

As part of this unfolding story, I will clearly explain to you how working toward critical success has changed my life. Please note, however, that what I will tell you should only serve as a guidepost. You are responsible for taking the information presented here and making it your own.

I can only serve as a guide. What I hope to teach you through my words, and the telling of my life experiences, is nothing more than self-empowerment. This book, and its supporting materials, are about realizing your true self, discovering your passion, and living your dream. It's about providing you with the tools you require in order to think clearly and define your own personal path to success.

Please understand that the majority of us are socialized against success as part of our place in this culture. We are trained from birth by successful people and organizations to be consumers, mice in the maze of life, the rat in the race. It requires effort and hard work to reverse this socialization, to break the training of our media-driven consumercelebreality culture. However, it can be done.

I want to tell you the truth. I want to tell you about how you've been using your money, how the *careless wealthy* have come to rely upon your money and your ignorance to fuel their empty lives. I say *careless* because I want to be specific. Not all wealthy people are vain, self-important, parasites on society. Many of the wealthy are critical thinkers and spend an inordinate amount of time and money seeking to solve the world's problems.

However, they can't save you. You have to save yourself. Only you can learn to use what's within you. Only you can pick yourself up and realize your potential. Only you can push yourself into realizing critical success. By thinking critically, you can achieve success and be satisfied with the results. You will have earned just as much or more than any mendicant *(this is not a big word – look it up)* rich boy, gnawing at the feet of his father's wealth like a rabid dog, dependent upon you and everyone like you to secure the future of his family's wealth.

Dismiss them. They aren't worth a thought. Most certainly do not dream of being like them. They are part and parcel to spoon culture.

Allow me to reiterate.

There is a lie in many of the seminars you attend. In this book I share with you the truth. I will tell you about the real estate seminars, the stock market schemes, and the people who make $35,000 in one month on one stock trade, or picked up a check at the closing table.

Know this: when you attend these seminars in droves, like the one recently held in my city, where people attended by the thousands, you're doing nothing more than putting your hard-earned money into someone else's pocket.

Again, let's be perfectly clear. I'm giving you information that you could find for yourself if you would only take the time to look for it. The same goes for the information provided in the seminars. The person who's telling you about how he made money in real estate did not get rich in real estate. He got rich because you bought his book, attended his seminars, and picked up his board game. I can't repeat this enough, because even though some of you know it, you go back to the poison well again and again and again. Stop drinking from the fount of absurdity. If his program made him so wealthy, WHY WOULD HE SHARE IT WITH YOU?

The person who's on television raving about how rich you're going to be when you start day trading is truly an apostate from hell. He will tell you how to use leverage and trade in options. He will tell you how to use a red-light/green-light program to know when to buy stocks, as I mentioned earlier. He will sell all this to you and ask you to subscribe to his newsletter and daily stock-picking list. All this will cost you a ream of cash. Some of you may make some money. The majority of you will go hopelessly broke and probably generate a mountain of debt and a new bad habit: day trading. The apostate will profit tremendously, taking home a horde of your hard-earned cash.

The person who's begging you to attend a seminar for a new program he's discovered and implores you to join this new group of serious, religious-minded people in a once-in-a-lifetime opportunity is not doing you a favor. You will go to the seminar. You will all pray together. You will pray to God and beg for prosperity. You will talk about the powerful new innovative products you're going to sell. You'll talk about generating your profits from home. You will pick up watch-words like *down-line* and *residual income*. You will spend money and time building your so-called business. You will try to recruit people. You will spend more money. You'll fly to another seminar. You'll spend more money. You'll see the presentations, where people are living in gated communities on golf courses, sailing in their yachts, and tooling around town in their brand new Hummers. Your eyes will shine like stars. You will see yourself incredibly rich in just a few short months. You'll recruit. You'll spend more money. Then the awful truth will settle in. You're in another pyramid scheme. Or you're in a valid multi-level marketing scheme, but you don't have the skill to recruit and move product. You'll realize you've spent $40,000 and don't have a thing to show for it

I'm only telling you the truth.

I want to clarify and ensure that you understand. It's all part of becoming a critical-thinker where wealth and money-making are concerned. Understand, you're making me wealthy when you buy my book. And for this, I truly thank you. This is my passion, and you are facilitating my success.

Maybe you'll never attend another seminar again. Maybe you'll go to some seminars but think critically about the opportunity being presented. If you do, then maybe you'll do your research, take your time, be cautious, and separate the lies from the truth. Who knows? Maybe it's your destiny to start your own seminar or multi-level marketing company, or bakery, or real-estate brokerage firm. The point is that through critical thinking, you will be able to see through the fabric of lies, the smoke-and-mirrors, and the fluff, no matter how it's presented. You'll be able to achieve critical success because you think and plan.

I'm not going to make you rich. I'm not going to have you thinking that by the time you've finished this book, you'll be well on your way to your first million. What I will do is generate hope and desire. I will do my best to inspire you, to light a fire in the engine of your mind, to open the door to self-empowerment and eventually true critical success, whatever that may mean for you as an individual.

Do you think you have what it takes? Read on and let's find out.

CHAPTER 2
THE PROPER MINDSET
AND THE BARRIERS

You're here. I am pleased. If you've found the information I presented in the introduction, and chapter one to your liking, then proceed at full speed, intrepid adventurer. As I said, I'm not going to make you rich. However, I will make you motivated. I will empower you, and I will provide you with the proper mindset and the requisite tools necessary to redefine yourself as an individual, ready and willing to employ the powers of the secret, the law of attraction, or whatever else you may discern on the path of your personal journey toward realizing true wealth.

Before we go further, I would like to make sure you are approaching this material with the proper frame of mind. I've mentioned the law of attraction and the secret. I often talk to the people around me about the power of thinking positively. Realizing critical success requires that you have an open mind and approach the possibilities that will open before you with a strong, healthy, positive attitude.

Every day, as I approach my work, I glance at an imperative I have pinned to my wall:

YOU'RE NOT BEGINNING TO
DO A GOOD JOB UNTIL YOU'VE
ASKED YOURSELF, "WHAT CAN I DO
BETTER TODAY?"

Now, the work for that day may be particularly grueling. It may be something wholly unpleasant, which I would like to avoid at all costs. However, if the work is necessary, I know I have to approach it in the right frame of mind. In order to be effective at this unpleasant task, I have to maintain a positive attitude. To help bolster that attitude, every morning I read a poem by Charles Swindoll called "Attitude." As an exercise, I want you to stop right now, and go look up this powerful, and inspirational poem. If you're near a computer, bring up a search engine, and search for it. If you're not near a computer, stop, and go find one. Trust me, this is important.

Once you've found the poem, and read it, read it again. I want you to consider the following:

- Have you considered the impact your attitude has on your life?
- Have you ever thought about what changing your attitude can do for you personally?
- Have you thought about the sheer power and impact your attitude has on other people?

How are you doing today? *I'm doing great!*

It's raining outside. You have a to pull a twelve-hour shift. They cut your pay. You might be laid off. How can you be doing great? *I have my affirmations. I have my beliefs. I have my faith. Today is a great day, for I am alive, and my life is full of possibilities. And you know what else? Tomorrow promises to be an even better day.*

This type of attitude from a friend or coworker can be irritating. However, you can observe how they approach life and learn from them. To me the poem "Attitude" is absolutely crucial to achieving critical success. This is how we work, people. This is how we move forward. This is how we achieve success. Read "Attitude" again, and again, and again.

I would like you to think of someone you consider successful.

Who comes to mind? Do you think of Oprah Winfrey? Does Bill Gates come to mind? What about Michael Dell? Do you know who Lakshmi Mittal is? What about Richard Parsons, Kenneth Chenault, and Stan O'Neal? Do you consider President Clinton a success or President Bush? What about your local physician? Do you consider the priest or pastor of your church successful? What about your local politicians (the honest ones)? How about your lawyer? I'm purposefully not mentioning any sports, movie, or television luminaries, excluding Oprah because she's almost a force of nature. I consider her a humanitarian and an activist as well as a big- and small-screen personality.

I need you to stop idolizing the avatars of our media-driven consumercelebreality culture. If you are meant to be one of them, then life will unfold for you in such a fashion that movies and soundstages become your reality. However, in order to understand if this was meant for you, if this is your passion, you need to think critically about yourself, your talent, what you're good at, and what you enjoy. You must discern *for yourself*, independent of external influences, if what you are currently working toward is what you were meant to do.

If you are breaking your back to become something and you truly enjoy it—if you smile every day at the attempt or if you struggle, fail, damn near suffer immense pain, but something inside of you still moves you towards this objective with a sense of joy—then my friends, you've found it. You have discovered your passion. You are doing your life's work. Let nothing, within reason, dissuade you from your goal.

<u>What are the characteristics of the critically successful?</u>

They are highly motivated.
Successful people have a plan.
They are highly focused.

Successful people look for solutions to problems.
Successful people have a strong work ethic.
Successful people have a very positive attitude about their work.

Do the above characteristics apply to you? Do you see yourself in those words? There are other words and phrases you can probably think of to describe successful people; however, I consider the above to be among the most critical. Think of successful people you're read about, heard about, or seen on television. The most successful can be described in the above terms. Now, again, I ask you, do the words describe you? If they do not, then it is time to make a change. You have come to a bend in the road. All you need to do is slow down, stop, think, and casually, courageously, walk around the bend toward a brighter future. Be what other successful people are.

Make your own luck, for it is nothing more than good preparation colliding headlong with opportunity at the crossroads of life.

Before we move on, can you think of some characteristics of unsuccessful people? Do they easily come to mind? As you mentally scroll through your list of words and phrases to describe the many failures you know around the corner, up the street, in your family, on the daily news, in your school, at your job, do you take pause at how much longer this list is? Do you find it fascinating that it is easy to think of the negative and we struggle with the positive? Do you feel conditioned for failure?

<u>What are the characteristics of unsuccessful people?</u>

Lazy
Little, or no motivation
Constant lack of focus
Scattered thoughts and ideas
Never plan
Consistently problem-centered
Not solution-oriented
Weak work ethic
Bad attitude, dwell on the negative

As some of you no doubt have noticed, essentially these characteristics are the opposite of what was listed for successful people. Unfortunately so many of us seem to lean toward these characteristics. Do you see yourself described in the words above? If you say no, are you being honest with yourself? At times we all display these characteristics. It's human to have a bad attitude. However, the question is whether or not you consistently have a bad attitude. It's basic. It's simple. If you want to be successful, you cannot be lazy. You must be motivated. You must have focus. You must know what you want to do and stick to it. You must have a plan. You cannot dwell on problems and must be able to come up with solutions. You must have a strong work ethic. You must have a good, positive attitude. When you feel your attitude about to shift and your confidence wavers, read the poem "Attitude." It never fails to give me a boost.

With the correct mindset, we can begin to tackle the task of creating critical success for ourselves in earnest. However, once we have the proper mindset, we must become aware of the forces arrayed against us. As an individual striving for critical success, you must understand what powers were at play that inhibited your growth and the realization of your true potential. There are barriers to critical success. What's interesting about the barriers is that they are at the very heart of our free enterprise engine of prosperity. However, for some time now they have been running on overdrive, stimulating minds and closing mental doors, making it that much harder for people to think for themselves. And why do you pay this exorbitant price? For what purpose does the jet fire its afterburners? Simple. It puts more product, more stuff, in your homes. You become mindless, and those who share in the creation of stuff become wealthier.

Please know and understand that there is nothing wrong with becoming wealthier. You want to become one of these people who share in the creation of stuff. However, as a culture, we have to ratchet the engine back a bit. We have to ease the throttle so that we can stop buying so much stuff and start concentrating on our individual growth, the realization of who we are as a people.

Your true identify is not wrapped up in your car, even though you may remind someone of a jeep. Your big house does not define you personally, even though you may be as big as one and dress like all the awful overpriced stuff you've managed to cram between its walls. The number of credit cards you have has no bearing on your ability to achieve. In fact, it may be indicative of your stupidity. These things are all part of why you are not, nor will be, successful, if you continue along this path. These material things do not represent your true passion, no matter how much you may want them to. I propose that those of you who believe in surrounding yourself with these material things are empty inside. Though you may pretend you are happy and have found your true calling, you have not. You are hollow. Your passion is a blowing wind across the vast wasteland of your soul, a place of unrealized dreams. What fuels this emptiness are the barriers to true critical success. They are at the core of our culture.

<u>What are the barriers?</u>

1) Lack of critical thinking skills
2) Media-driven consumercelebreality
3) The willful assumption of debt
4) Getting-rich-quick goals

Consider this: if the above barriers are at the core of our culture, how can we ever prosper? The answer to this question is simple. We can't. As an individual in society struggling and striving to realize your full potential, you will never succeed in your quest if you continue to fall victim to these barriers. They are pervasive, they are infectious, and they are truly destructive to middle- and lower-class prosperity. You must learn to recognize and understand them. You must learn to see them and not ignore them but rather acknowledge them for what they are and use them to your advantage. Let their very existence motivate you and drive you toward critical success.

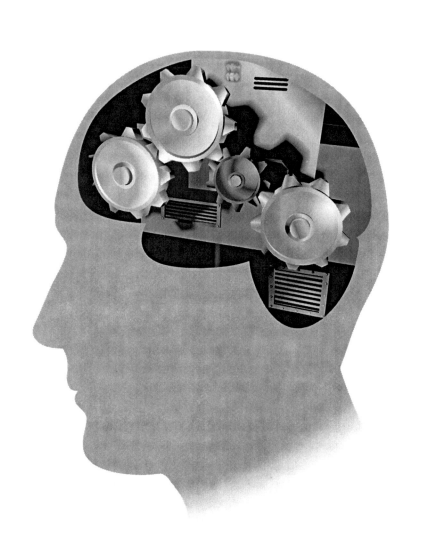

CHAPTER 3
THE LACK OF
CRITICAL THINKING

Of the four barriers, I think the most important to consider is the first. People don't think. No, it's more than this, people seem to have an overwhelming desire to not think. We talk down to people who try to excel. We say things like, *why do you like to read so much?* We use words like *geek* and *nerd*. I—yes, me, your author—am a geek. I'm not a nerd, because I'm not, nor was I ever, that bright in regard to academic achievement. I couldn't cut the mustard when it came to grades. I'll tell you, I wasn't thinking critically about my future and how much better things would be for me if I just paid attention and studied. I'll tell you something else. I was jealous of the smart ones, the ones who consistently made As.

If only I knew then what I know now, things would have been different. However, it's never too late to start. That is part of the message I sincerely wish to impart to you. Start thinking critically today. Start by just slowing down and finally coming to a halt. Start by stopping. Consider who you are and where you are in life. Then start thinking critically about it; question yourself, wonder where you want to be. Wonder who you want to be.

Understand that as a society we seem to admire the stupid and inane, putting them on pedestals and adoring their celebrity. People, understand that being sloppily fat, in mind and body, with bags of fiddle-faddle lodged on your stomach or between your man-breasts, vacantly staring at the television, watching the plastic lives of the low-brow rich and famous, is absolutely no way to go through life.

You are throwing your potential into the dirt on the side of the road. You are letting it twist in the wind. You are completely abandoning the exuberant and vibrant person that exists deep within you, the person that holds the key to your passion. You're abandoning him or her for the plastic people, the people who mean nothing to themselves, let alone you. It's time to start thinking critically, people. More importantly, it's time to start thinking critically about who you are and how you will achieve critical success.

Lack of critical thinking skills is an extremely important barrier to consider. If you do not break through it, you will not achieve success. Why is this barrier so important? Stop, think about it, and consider it.

Critical thinkers know and understand personal accountability. However, I'll make this easy for you. If you want to achieve, you have to be ready to be accountable for all your actions. You must start here and now to take responsibility for your lot in life. You must be able to examine yourself and understand the difference between what you've done and what was done to you. You also must be able to understand what you have not done and why that has inhibited your growth.

For instance, if you don't understand what the word *inhibit* means, you must be accountable for your lack of understanding. No one is going to force you to understand the word. This situation starts from a sad low and proceeds downhill. Can you understand the word? Can you not discern its meaning from how it's being used in the sentence? Can you not figure it out from the context? Did you not learn this skill in school? Do you blame it on the teachers and their lack of educating you responsibly? Do you blame it on your parents and their lack of parenting? Stop. Do you not blame it on yourself? Stop. Think. You're an individual. If no one is going to help you, you have to take the first step. This, people, is personal accountability. If you don't understand what *inhibit* means, go pick up the dictionary and look up the definition. Read the definition. Understand the definition. Go back to my sentence and reread it. Now does it make sense? This was a simple example. Being personally accountable is not always an easy thing. In fact, it can be one of the hardest things you ever do. However, I guarantee you will experience a strong sense of satisfaction when you're able to hold your head up, and say, *I am responsible for this. It was entirely up to me. I made the decision. I acted.* Whether it was a good thing or a bad thing, it was your thing. You are accountable.

WHAT IS CRITICAL THINKING?

1. The act or practice of one that thinks with careful, exact evaluation, and judgment. 2. Indispensable, and essential cognition. 3. To consider, anticipate a possible action as a result of careful analysis and evaluation.

Some of you may not know what cognition is. So what is cognition?

1.The mental process of knowing, which includes perceiving, recognizing, conceiving, judging, reasoning, and imagining.

For more information please go to the following website:
www.criticalthinking.org

Thinking critically requires you to question yourself. Are you responsible? Being responsible means you are accountable for you actions. However, you must ask yourself questions before you embark on a course of action, because you want to be accountable for something good. Do you indulge in irresponsible behavior? Before you act, do you ask yourself, *is this stupid?*

Some of you people out there tend toward the extreme. *I want to be a real estate agent. I'll start next week with the money I make from robbing this store.* People, somebody help me here. I swear to you there are people around you every day who think like this. *If I take a little bit of money from the discretionary fund, it will be okay. After all, I put in all those extra hours.* No, it is not okay. You're committing a crime. Did you ask yourself any reasonable questions? Did you think critically about the possible results of your actions: termination, incarceration, shame, and ridicule? Oh yeah, if you get caught, you don't have to worry about personal accountability. The legal system will take care of that.

These examples are extreme, but I'm trying to make a point. Bringing it back to something more of you understand, consider stopping, thinking, and asking yourself a few questions before you go buy that new car or ten new outfits, complete with shoes, or that stupid-looking gaudy ring on your finger, or those ridiculously overpriced rims on your car. You want to be successful? It starts with being responsible with what you already have. Don't squander what you have on the crap you don't need.

You want to be successful? You've committed to it? What's your plan? Too many of us go through our lives wandering aimlessly. We don't have a plan. Critical thinkers plan strategically, for the long vision, and tactically, for the immediate, the here and now. They adjust their plans according to a given situation. They think about what they're doing and move forward in life confident in the fact that in time they will achieve their objective. They're methodical when necessary, dogged, and determined. However, they know when to adjust, to ratchet it back and take it easy. They may even stop working on the plan for a while, just because the mind and body need a break. However, they establish goals. They see a road—a road paved with gold bricks and it leads to their eventual objective, their own personal critical success.

For the most part, we as a society are not critical thinkers. We lack the skill and we don't even want to take the time to try to develop it. We don't read a great deal; nor do we desire to do so. We no longer want to stretch our minds, push our limits, or examine ourselves to try to determine what we, as individuals, can truly achieve. We don't like to work on being better. And throughout this entire lackadaisical dance, we maintain a nasty attitude. We lament our lack of achievement. We hate those who look better and achieve more than we do. We languish in our fat bodies and fat minds, and look in the mirror and complain about why the world has done this to us. *Why won't anybody help me out?* We pray to God for wealth and prosperity. Yet we won't lift a finger to do anything about it for ourselves. It's so much easier to let the books gather dust, to let the season pass us by; let the mind rot into senility and the man-breasts grow to ginormous proportions, as we imbibe *Springer,* and *Girls Gone Wild.*

Still, when the real estate, stock, and inventor commercials come on, we sit forward just a bit, letting the chips fall down the mountainous slopes of our ginormous breasts and belly onto the dirty carpet next to our crusty feet, and dream of mansions, boats, and six-figure automobiles in six months. Question nothing. We buy the packet, DVDs, cassettes, tapes, and guide. Go to the seminar. Learn nothing and end up right back on the couch, with chips between our man-breasts, asking ourselves, *why me?*

It starts here. It starts now. Break the cycle. Question everything. However, more importantly, start by questioning yourself. Break through this barrier and work yourself toward the clear.

That was a heavy barrier.

It's thick and dense and requires a great deal of effort and hard work to overcome. You may not be able to do it alone. Nothing will prevent you from reaching out to others, expressing your views, and having a dialogue. However, having a clear understanding of the other barriers will arm you in being able to pierce through that which holds you back.

The next barrier, media-driven consumercelebreality is truly the soul of a nation, going far beyond geographic boundaries, patriotic ties of country, and ecumenical ties of faith. This barrier is only able to thrive because we don't think. The moment you begin to think, you will have the strength to pierce through this diseased barrier. Thankfully, this pervading force of mindlessness has not penetrated to our cultural core. People still believe in the might of a unified nation. So what is this nation? The nation is the nameless faceless millions of the TV Nation. Understand, this nation goes beyond generations. It includes those who eat at the table of multiple forms of media, as do we all, be it the Internet, movies, radio, magazines, or newspapers. Wherever a message can get pumped into our brains, is where you will find the citizens of this nation. They are the infected.

Are you a member of this nation? You probably are. I once was. If you are still a member of this nation, let me explain to you how to opt out and abandon your citizenship. It goes back to the first barrier. If you see a few commercials and they successfully get you to understand that life not only takes VISA but also a new leased vehicle and a new wardrobe because your store is having the *bomb* sale, then you are a card-carrying member of TV nation. Stop! Think! Ask yourself a few questions.

I just paid off that department store credit card at 22 percent. Do I really need a new wardrobe?

I've been finally made to understand that picking up a leased vehicle is one of the stupidest things an individual can do. Do I really want to be labeled a spoon?

The credit cards, the credit cards! Do I need to buy my groceries on credit or even debit? If I pause and have to think about the purchase, do I really need the chocoblock megasugar pops for me or my kid? I'm fat enough as it is.

Just asking these questions will help you abandon your citizenship in TV Nation. You're thinking critically about your situation and discerning between wants and needs. If you concentrate on your needs now, put together a strong plan, and only indulge your wants every once in while, then you will find success in time and be able to possibly purchase all the things you truly want.

So how do we define media-driven consumercelebreality?

CHAPTER 4
MEDIA-DRIVEN
CONSUMERCELEBREALITY

WHAT IS MEDIA-DRIVEN CONSUMERCELEBREALITY?

1. A social trend in which the factors of production, distribution, and most importantly marketing, come together to facilitate successful economic growth at the expense of the consumer.

The definition is simple enough to understand. You are the consumer. Corporations, partnerships, and even sole-proprietors that advertise fund the marketing. Our society's marketing engine is a massive beast, and it facilitates the social trend. They push candy-colored commercials into your mind in order to promote your desire to push candy-colored crap down your throat and into your system.

However, understand this clearly. Though the companies do bear some responsibility, the lion's share (and by this I mean almost all of it), the decision rests in your hands. By thinking critically you can defy the affects of media-driven consumercelebreality. It's really simple. Do you stop and ask yourself if you really need those new shoes, that now outfit, that overpriced piece of jewelry, that leased car, or that mini-mansion, which you can only afford with an interest-only loan? Think, people. You have to think.

Media-driven consumercelebreality, or MDC, is the systemic disease our culture uses to get you into the department stores. It is the sum result of the pervasiveness of pop life, the popular life, the life of the celebrity, which far too many of us seek to emulate: a life of emptiness, filled with platinum baubles, the material things, cars, and Cristal. Many of us simple people become consumed with this foolishness. How can we hope to handle the onslaught of pop life when celebrities crash and burn every day? MDC, in part, perpetuates this way of life. It feeds an economic model that is geared toward making the consumer consume more and more things. It convinces us that true happiness is the acquisition of large amounts of stuff. MDC, as it now stands, is bloated and expansive. It is growing, confusing, and confounding, and every day it alters the consumer's mind.

How does MDC alter one's mind?

This one point is crucial. It's why I coined the term. People buy what they *think* they need, not what they need. MDC drives you toward the belief that you are your own celebrity. Now, there's nothing wrong with thinking you're special. You are. You should know that you're a great person. However, do you really want to be a celebrity, as we have come to understand the term?

People know they need food. They know they need shelter. They value their health. People clearly understand what survival mandates. We acquire the things we truly need to survive through human interaction and relationships that are personal, financial, and industrial.

Once our needs are adequately satisfied, we move into the area of quality of life. We seek to satisfy our wants. This is a good thing. Through what we have earned, through what is produced, through our relationships, we can acquire things that make our lives more pleasant, more interesting. One of the things we can acquire is access to entertainment.

People have always been moved by the mindless. We are at our best when we seek to expand our minds, to learn and grow. This too is entertaining. However, even the best of us sometimes like to watch entertainment that has no redeeming value whatsoever.

As our world progressed, we became more expansive in how we might be entertained. Opportunities to generate income on goods and services are directly tied to how we entertain ourselves.

Mediums to convey information have been around for as long as there was a something to tell, whether it was about updates from the war front, new laws, or the victor in the latest gladiatorial games. As we have progressed, so to have our mediums. We send information through signs, song, newspapers, billboards, movies, television, placards, pamphlets this, that, and the other. We are constantly inventing ways to tell the tale and get you to purchase something in relation to the tale.

And one day, in our genius, we invented an industry around this need. We invented ... marketing!

What is the goal of marketing? I tell you now the goal of marketing is to change your mind. Its sole purpose is to alter what you're thinking to the benefit of the client the people who want to sell you stuff. The marketing companies have become incredibly effective at doing this. They are constantly convincing you to buy things you don't need. They're so good at it you can't even tell when they're working you over.

In America we have turned marketing into a high art form. Everything is for sale, as well as how we sell it and what medium the advertising will take. We see people in our mediums that are glamorous and possess a lot of stuff. The marketing machine has convinced the majority of us that we need to be just like the people we see in these mediums: magazines, television, and the movies.

We've gone way beyond necessities. Some of us have become so taken in by this need to be like the person on television that we neglect our personal needs. We don't expand our minds. We don't read. We don't think—beyond needing something platinum-plated or designer-made. We live to buy things. We need to look like our favorite celebrity. We thrive on what people think about us, and what we wear, where we live, and what we drive. We need them to look at us, admire us; want to be like us, to *be* us, to be the imaginary celebrity.

Understand, I want stuff too. Really, I do. I just want to wait until I can afford it. Do some of you want to do the same? If you don't, then you should. You need to stop! Right now, you need to stop!

Stop and think, people. Abandon this need to embrace the pop life. Understand that stars are up in the sky. Hollywood stars are people just like you and me. They get out of bed, just like you. They put on pants, just like you. However, their pants may cost four hundred dollars. That's their choice. Do you need four-hundred-dollar jeans? Your ass is covered, right? And does your ass look good in your jeans? Even if it doesn't, the point is, if you think about it, you can probably think of something better to do with your four hundred dollars, like putting it in an investment fund.

When you feed into the social trend, you aim your mind toward emptiness and mediocrity. I believe this powerful push toward the accumulation of crap is at the center of our society's drive toward mediocrity. We want to purchase more crap and more idiot boxes (televisions), on which we can see more crap being pushed at us. We get stuck in front of the idiot box, and lose our zest for life.

The third barrier is really the steel struts in the concrete of the other barriers. It winds its way though them all, picking away at your mental resolve, spurred on by your lackadaisical attitude and your refusal to think, fueled by media-driven consumercelebreality. It is the willful assumption of debt, and it has literally killed people. It's a life-taker and a heartbreaker. People put bullets in their heads and swallow bottles of pills because they've mismanaged their wealth. It ruins relationships, tears marriages apart, and brings mighty nations to ruin. We endure all this death and destruction because we can't manage our pocketbooks.

CHAPTER 5
THE WILLFUL
ASSUMPTION OF DEBT!

We create monumental barriers to critical
success by leveraging our futures today.
We need to be saving our money, investing our money,
and using our money for future prosperity. We must stop
using all we earn on shiny things, the floss and flash.

Shopping has become an American pastime, to our general detriment. For those of us living in America, we imagine ourselves living at the pinnacle of human achievement. It is not a false assumption. Never in human history have people lived as well as we Americans. I'm talking in general. I'm not referring to overweight, sociopathic monarchs with inane visions of divinity.

Debt has become the American way of life. It's now one of our most hallowed pastimes. As opposed to building our savings, we glory in finding new and fascinating ways to spend our hard-earned cash. We love to see the look of envy, be it real or imagined, in our friends' or neighbors' eyes when we drive by in our brand new automobiles. Of course, we don't talk about the heated pain we experience in the dark watches of the night, dwelling on the mounting stacks of envelopes spread all over the table downstairs, bills that are thirty, sixty, ninety days past due—and the big one, the bank threatening to foreclose on the house—all because we couldn't control ourselves, because we lacked discipline, because we couldn't think critically about the choices we were making, because we fell victim to MDC.

The act of shopping drives the engine of our economy. It makes America great. We produce things. Well, we don't produce as much as we used to. It's more accurate to say we design things, serve things, and sell things. We leave it up to other economies to actually make things.

However, this consumer-driven beast we've created always needs to grow. It's always looking for the next thing to sell. The insidiousness of media-driven consumercelebreality facilitates its growth. If we continue down this path, the fall of America will be a foregone conclusion.

Some say it's already too late.

It doesn't have to be this way. We don't have to remain a nation of spendthrifts. We can once again be a nation of people who save. For those of you who live in other countries, be wary of the forces currently acting upon you. For those countries that are growing in economic power, don't allow the growing reach of MDC to transform your people into platinum sycophants, worshipping at the altar of material greed.

A point of order: Shopping is a good thing. Stores employ people. Stores sell products. Products are grown or manufactured, distributed, and set up for retail consumption. Stores pay people to sell you these products. People use the money they earn to buy stuff from the store they work in, as well as other stores. People pay for services, such as dental cleaning, dry-cleaning, movie entertainment, sports events, concerts, etc.

This is the cycle, people. It is the true engine. The more efficient the engine, the more it produces and the stronger the economy. However, in a desire to seek evermore profits, people think up ways to not only bring their products to you with the utmost efficiency but also figure out how to make you buy more products, even if it's far more than you need. This adds value to their corporate bottom line. They make more revenue. The shareholders are happy. Stock prices go up. People get richer and richer, but not the people working at the cash register. They don't know about this part of the cycle.

What they do know is that they have a desire. What they don't know is that they've been infected by MDC. MDC makes them want more and more of what's out there for sale. Even if they don't really need it, they want it. They don't think critically. They barely think at all. They spend all their hard-earned money on four overpriced tires and some ridiculous-looking rims. They put it on a used car that a friend around the corner painted candy red, and which costs less than the tires and wheels. They ride to work, thinking they are superstars, with no money in the bank.

These people tip the scales toward disaster, and people who control the factors of production push it along, heedless of where we'll all eventually end. We have not figured out how to achieve balance.

We produce more than we need. We haven't taken the time to figure out how to achieve economic balance, producing what we need and at the same time satisfying a profit motive for those who generate the ideas. We equate prosperity with profits. We abuse the factors of production, the people, and the resources in order make more and more stuff.

We happily spread MDC far and wide, infecting the culture with stupidity, driving people into the stores to spend, spend, spend. People are people and can easily be deluded when not trained properly. If they don't have the tools with which to protect themselves, if they can't raise a mental shield before the onslaught of MDC, they hopelessly fall victim. They become consumer-beast prey. They don't save. They spend, spend, spend. They grow older and need, need, need. They strain society. They abdicate responsibility. They burden us all simply because they didn't think. They merrily dance their way through life buying crap they don't need, burning through cash as though it truly did grow on trees. Even while they complain about not having enough, they happily spend what they do have. They save nothing. *This* is the *willful assumption of debt*, and it is a killer.

Before we know it, we have taken on so much debt, that we can't sleep at night. We become irritable. We cry in the lonely watches of the night because we're afraid of what might happen when the sun rises.

Make no mistake, people; this is serious. Research it for yourselves. People literally snap under the overwhelming weight of debt. They steal. They commit murder. They commit suicide. They become irrational because they cannot pay for the ridiculous number of overpriced things they have bought with their available cash and credit, and the equity in their homes.

In the end they have leveraged their very futures for the floss and flash they cannot truly afford today. They assume massive loads

of debt, trying to be something they are not.

This is where critical thinking must come into play. We must be able to question ourselves at the moment of impulse. Some of us do quite well until we're faced with the purchase in our face. Then, on impulse, we go on a spending spree.

Right now, at this moment, I would like you to take the time to go back and read what is under *The Willful Assumption of Debt*. We, the people of the modern, prosperous world, are without a doubt a consumer-oriented culture. We do indeed love to live the pop life. We spend most of our time dreaming about the stuff we want to accumulate, the stuff we definitely will accumulate, and how good we'll look in it after we've accumulated it. Whether it's a car, clothes, jewelry, or an expensive home, we spend an inordinate amount of time dwelling on what we want and what we get.

Then we proceed to spend an inordinate amount of time fretting about how we're going to pay for it. Why do we fret? We fret because most of us have purchased our shiny, flossy, flashy stuff on credit. We truly do leverage our futures on the needless crap we buy today.

Life does not take credit! You don't need Visa, MasterCard, or Amex to thrive, let alone survive. It would behoove us to all become informed consumers, discerning purchasers, informed buyers. Before we know it, our lack of discipline will close off the opportunity to pay by the means which we choose and force us down the path to card systems only. Understand, Visa definitely makes life easier. However, if you haven't yet learned discipline, plastic is more than a hindrance, more than just a barrier. It's a concrete wall, a steel ball and chain weighing you down, holding you back from what can and should be yours, true critical success.

You, as an individual striving for your own personal, passionate, critical success, must break the chain and smash through this barrier. You cannot do it without faith. You cannot do it without discipline. You cannot do it without a plan. And, most importantly, you cannot do it without thinking. To make it twice as nice, don't just think about it; think about it critically. Question yourself, question your circumstance, question what you want, question what you have, question what you need. Think, plan, decide. You do not need to keep up with the Joneses, Smiths, Harrisons, Wangs, or Cortezes. You need to stop caring about what they have and be thankful for what is yours. And as for what you want—what you really want—stop, think about it, consider it, and if you do truly want it and you visualize it as part of your future, it will come to you in time. It will be yours. It will be part of your success story.

For those of you that have marshaled the strength to at least partially break through the other barriers, this fourth barrier is especially for you. Many of us make the decision that we're going try something. We've already covered this ground, but we'll go over it again and again so that you understand that you must approach this barrier with a discerning eye, a critical eye. Many of us decide that we're ready to create wealth. We're fueled by MDC. Sometimes we're fueled by an honest desire to succeed. Whatever it is, we decide that we're ready to work, and we want to strive for our own champagne wishes and caviar dreams. Unfortunately most of us reach for the opportunity that is thrust in our faces, and often enough, this is not what will open the door to our own yellow brick road. What we're simply doing is falling for more floss and flash in our race to acquire glitz and glamour. We fall prey to the get-rich-quick scheme.

$uccess

CHAPTER 6
THE GET-RICH-
QUICK SCHEMES

In every lie there is a modicum of truth. The truth is the light and propels you forward; the lie holds you steadfast and will eventually force you backward. Be wary of the lie and seek the truth.

In every lie there is a modicum of truth. Still, the lie is so great as to be almost all encompassing. What am I talking about? I'm talking about the commercials, the newspaper ads, the fliers, the radio spots, even the billboards, all telling you to take advantage of your opportunity today. What is the Great Lie?

The Great Lie is that you can get rich, and relatively quickly, by following someone else's specific plan, joining their specific group, or selling their specific product or service.

What is the truth? The truth is that someone may very well get rich, most notably the person who started the idea. Yes, this person will become rich, as well as some of the people who joined under him, and perhaps a few industrious followers, those who already have an innate talent they are utilizing. What is that talent? They are born sellers.

What is the lie? The lie is that the people who push the scheme your way are conning you. They are altering your perceptions and playing on your emotions. They may not even come right out and say that you will get rich, each and every one of you, but they are selling you an emotion, a belief, that if you do what they say, pay good money for the program and packets, CDs, DVDs, books, and tapes they are hawking, then you will get rich. It's a good free-market economy model. Multi-level marketing works. Just look at Amway. It's phenomenal. Still, Amway's is most certainly not for everyone. In fact, it can ruin many of your relationships. Quite a few people find it very distasteful when you try to turn them into customers or recruits.

However, you have to determine if any of these opportunities are truly for you. You can make this determination without spending your money again and again and again. When you do this, you are considered a certain type of person, not just a spoon.

I'll tell you later.

Here's a bit of honesty before we move forward. I'm selling you my ideas along the same lines as these other concepts. What's different? I'll make it as plain as I can, as simple as I can. Read the following words and burn them into your mind.

I am not going to make you rich.

That's not my job. I won't tell you a lie, and guarantee you that I can open the door to financial wealth and riches. What I do have is a passion for creating. I desire to know and understand things. At this moment I desire to know and understand why we're so fiscally irresponsible. It is my passion and truest desire to be part of a solution that corrects this situation in our society.

I'm not going to make you monetarily rich. However, if you read what I have to offer and follow the guidelines, and utilize the tools I present, then perhaps you will become wealthy. You may even become monetarily rich. It's entirely up to you. The same holds true for these other programs. However, I'm not going to lie to you up front and tell you riches are coming your way in six months. You can become rich, but the responsibility lies with you.

I'll give you one guarantee.

Once you're done reading my material, you will want to become a critical thinker, striving for critical success, armed and ready to determine what that success is for you as an individual.

There, that's the best I can do. And if you read that statement and truly understand, you'll know deep down inside that it's more than enough. It's all you'll ever need.

Now let's expose the lies.

The Multi-Level Marketing Lie

The day I started working on this section of the book, I had just seen a television story on a multi-level marketing company that was selling sugar pills to people in order to promote health. This story really touched me. At its heart was the tale of a young woman who had lost her mother to a hemorrhage and her father to a brain tumor. She had been diagnosed with a brain tumor as well.

The doctors operated on her and removed most of the brain tumor. However, they had to leave some of it behind or risk paralyzing her. The next step in her treatment was to receive radiation and chemotherapy. However, she had other plans. She read about this company selling these sugar pills, which she believed would cure her cancer.

Yes, she believes a sugar pill will cure her cancer.

Now, I'll be honest with you, I don't know everything. I don't claim to know everything. In fact, I believe I will never know enough. In the world of medicine and human health, we all still have a great deal to learn. Our brains and bodies are powerful. I can't say that through belief, strong will, and a sugar pill that motivates said belief, she won't *will* what remains of her tumor out of existence. It might happen. Doctors like to refer to it as a placebo effect. Unfortunately I don't think the odds are in her favor.

Her doctors told her that if she were their child, they would force her to take the radiation and chemotherapy. The CEO of this multi-level marketing company even said in the television interview that his sugar pill is not meant to substitute for a doctor's advice but plays a part in the overall health equation.

I don't really know what that means.

I wish this young girl well and I am truly praying for her. I know cancer, as do many of us. There have been people in my family who have suffered its ravages and lost their lives. There have been those who beat cancer and claim the title of survivor. I believe this girl is courageous. However, I also think she's being irresponsible. I hope and pray this ends well.

Why am I telling you about this company, which I will not name? Simple. It's a multi-level marketing company that's actually listed on the NASDAQ stock exchange. The CEO is a multi-millionaire who lives in a fabulous mansion. His wife has written a book about the divinity and truth of his accomplishments. They are living in the lap of luxury. They embody caviar wishes and champagne dreams. They are what we aspire to and gravitate toward when we feel we are ready to pursue building wealth.

In a desire to get there quickly, we throw away all the traditional methods of saving money and investing. We see the videos, we hear the testimonials, and we just know for sure that we can do it too. We can be rich too. This is what this company is selling to its sales force.

The company itself does not claim to cure any diseases, let alone erode a tumor in the brain. However, strangely enough, its sales force actively trains its associate to aggressively pitch their sugar pill as a cure-all. It cures cancer. It cures AIDS. It cures fibromyalgia. People, this is unconscionable.

What really shocked me was watching a hidden-camera video of sales associates at one of this company's conventions. The room was packed with people just like you and me seeking to create personal wealth. The man, a high-level sales associate, was asking people to name a target market for their sugar pill. People in the audience, people like you and me, called out diseases like cancer, diabetes, and autism. Autism? A sugar pill can cure autism? The real truth wasn't the point. Their truth was that you can sell product to these people. The company does not openly promote this type of behavior, but it's happening nonetheless, whether they claim responsibility for it or not.

These people approached a woman with a beautiful Down syndrome child and told her this sugar pill would cure her child. They explained that this nutritional supplement, *sugar*, would actually change her facial appearance. Thankfully this woman was outraged and drove them off. Obviously she is not ruled by emotional stupidity. She's rational. She thinks. It doesn't even take critical thinking, people. Sugar can't perform plastic surgery, molding and altering facial features.

Understand me, my friends; there is a special place in hell for the people of this company. They are selling false hope, pain, and suffering. When you are lost and without any answers, you may very well reach for anything that offers a ray of hope. If you go online and hundreds of people are saying that a sugar pill can cure cancer, you'll probably buy the pill. I probably would too.

We have to demand that we all become critical thinkers, discerning consumers, responsible for our own healthcare when we can be. On the other side, we don't need people preying on us when we are near death and hope is all we have. We don't need people using our sincere desire and need to live a long life to fuel their dreams of a nine-room mansion and a Hummer.

As you go through this chapter on getting rich quick, I want you to consider what type of person you're going to be. Are you going to be a critical thinker? Will you truly consider and question? Will you come to the end of this chapter and say, *Yes, I will look, but I won't leap. I will be informed and perhaps walk.* Will you aspire to be the best you that you can be in order to achieve your own personal success? If this is your plan, then read on. However, know that with this responsibility must come some morality. I cannot abide people such as the sales associates from this sugar pill company. As I said, in hell, there is a place. Old Scratch is waiting for them, and I'm sure he has, oh, such plans.

Multi-level marketing companies are an old tried-and-true means of convincing people they will get rich. First allow me say to that MLMs are not evil. The people that run some of these enterprises may have some morality problems, but you'll find that in any field. A good strong MLM has a good, strong, quality product. The company has logistics. The company has strong communications. It has infrastructure. It has a good marketing plan. It is truly a legitimate company, not some fly-by-night, flung-together conman's scheme that won't stand up under the simplest scrutiny.

A good MLM company is following a sound business plan. It has **FOUND** a product. It **FOCUSES** on developing the product, researching the ins and outs and what impact it will have on the marketplace. The company has determined the product's intrinsic value, what it might sell for, and any other pertinent details that might come to mind.

This good MLM then **establishes the FUNDAMENTALS**. What are these fundamentals? They are the coherent details for activities based on the research developed when they were focusing on the product. They continued to define the fundamentals and derived actions steps, or tasks. These tasks become their plan. Once they were clear on the plan, they **EXECUTED!**

There are people out there who have become very, very wealthy through multi-level marketing. YES, THEY GOT RICH!

Maybe you can get rich through an MLM. However, you have to do your research. You have to examine each MLM opportunity that comes your way critically. As you conduct your analysis, know that a great many MLMs are true money-makers for all involved—at the beginning.

Allow me to stress this point: YOU CAN POSSIBLY MAKE A GREAT DEAL OF MONEY AT THE BEGINNING.

Those individuals who get in on the MLM opportunity at the beginning are literally at the top of the pyramid. Depending on the MLM opportunity, they will get most, if not all, of the rewards.

The individuals who start these MLM companies really make a great deal of money. THEY GET PAID at your expense. Understand, you're coming in at the tail end of the project, after it has been to twelve cities, and hosted twenty-two seminars in your city alone, with a hundred people at each seminar. Your chances of making money are fairly limited.

Residual income, residual income, you always hear people talk about residual income, money you can make while you sit comfortably on your ass. Downline, downline, you can make money through your downline, the people you recruit beneath you. They can sell your products while you sit happily collecting checks.

That's great for the people at the top, the people who started the company. It's not so great for you good folks in seminar twenty-three in city thirteen. I've been to several seminars and participated in many MLMs. I've been rewarded once. Still, I don't recall shaking the hand of a single person who was truly making money—not one. The person making money was always in the seminar video. The person doing the seminar usually had one check stub from a check he received for $350,000 that he flashed around to those particular individuals he thought had potential (to make you feel special).

There are people out there getting rich in MLMs. I've never met them personally, but I have read about them. I've actually met people who have made some good money in MLMs, but they don't quit their day jobs, and they certainly don't have yachts, and drive Ferraris. Still, I have met some who have done very well selling Mary Kay and Amway. However, they didn't make it by building downlines. They were sellers. They sold and sold and sold, and were able to build downlines by showing and telling. They were the truth and the people they recruited could see it, and become it.

If you find a legitimate MLM opportunity, you have to ask yourself, can you do this? Can you sell?

This, my friends, is what is at the heart of the MLM truth. Can you sell product? Can you sell juices? Can you sell water purifiers? Can you sell vacuum cleaners? Can you sell long-distance and voice-over-the-internet-phone service? Are you going to commit the time necessary to beat the streets and, through emotion, tone, and grasp of the material, use your own personal powers of persuasion (a little MDC) to convince people to buy what you're selling and then sell the idea to others and recruit them beneath you?

The best seller can feel his way through a pool of potential customers and convince them that toilet paper is the most important thing in the world (and for some of us, it is) and that they must buy their paper from him because the paper he's selling is the very best for your hard-earned dollar.

If you have considered it, if you have questioned yourself, if you have thought about it critically and have determined that this is you, then by all means, go find your MLM opportunity and make it happen.

I just saw a commercial for a new scheme on television. It had an animal as its spokesperson and hired actors to talk about how they made thousands of dollars in weeks. They actually had small type at the bottom of the screen saying these were paid actors!

Just remember, steer clear of sugar pills, gas pills (one of the guys involved in this scam is in jail), Nigerian schemes, and other such nonsense. Be a critical thinker. Question everything. And have a moral center. Remember, Old Scratch is waiting.

So You Wanna Be in Real Estate?

I'm going to tell you this, and I want you to pay very close attention. I want your eyes scrutinizing the letters in these words. I want this one scorched in your insides. No-money-down deals, foreclosure flipping, and tax lien property purchases are all real. You can make a great deal of money in these fields. However—and this is the important part—you have to truly determine if this is the passion you've been searching for. Is this truly the way you will be able to build wealth? Is this how you will achieve your very own personal critical success? So you want to buy a real estate program.

Know this: **THESE PROGRAMS ARE CRAP!**

Yes, I wrote it, I said it, and I'll say it again. These programs are crap. Now, I didn't say they weren't useful. I didn't say you couldn't learn from them. You can definitely learn from them. There is useful information in the guides, manuals, DVDs, CDs, tapes, and brochures. Unfortunately not all of it is useful, and a lot of it you can learn for free by conducting your own research on the Internet and checking out books from your local library. You could even buy a book or two.

The one thing you have to remember is this: you must be a critical thinker and a very discerning consumer. These people are just like the multi-level marketers. They need you to shell out your hard-earned dollars for their product. It's how they've built their wealth. They didn't get rich buying and selling real estate. However, they did become extremely wealthy when you all started buying their intellectual property. Teaching you how to buy and sell is extremely lucrative.

Don't get mad. Don't be upset if you've bought four real estate programs by four different people and spent two thousand dollars on an educational packet at a seminar where you spent fifty to gain entrance. Yes, you were a complete spoon, a sucker, along with eight thousand other spoons, sitting gleefully in your seats, listening to speaker after speaker charming you and convincing you to part with your money. Hey, it's just business. And yes, it was your fault because you weren't thinking clearly or critically. You were blinded by the allure of being rich by this time next year.

The four real estate programs are in the corner gathering dust, along with the tapes, CDs, and DVDs. The only thing you tossed in the trash is the pamphlet. As for the program, you keep thinking that since you paid for it, you might as well keep it, and it might actually come in handy one day. You're deluded. Yes, you wasted your money. Yes, there are gems in the dung that are your manuals. NO, YOU'RE NOT FOCUSED. Question: is this your passion? If it's your passion and you become *focused,* then you're halfway there. You really need to establish the *fundamentals* and *execute* your plan. Is that too hard? Do you really want to make it work?

Know this truth: real estate is for everyone. By this I mean we all, each and every one of us, deserves to own a home. Your home can serve you well. On paper it may represent the largest accumulation of wealth you possess. However, personally I don't consider your home a part of your wealth picture. Why? Because you live in it. It's where you rest your head. It keeps the rain off your back and protects you from the elements. It's where you experience life and love. Yes, it may represent wealth, but its more than that. People, your house is your home. Despite today's popular trend, it is not a smart thing to treat your home like a treasure chest, using its equity, which you've diligently built over time, to buy new stuff. You home is not an ATM.

Some people might use the equity in their homes to finance their entrepreneurial dreams. They may use their equity to finance a new business, purchasing inventory or securing a location. Some may use their equity to finance the purchase of rental property. I don't recommend doing this. Some people do this and they're successful. Some of them have very good plans. Others have no plan, a lot of faith, and a good strong hustle, and they make it through good 'ole fashioned chutzpah. Most people who do this fall flat on their faces, lose their investment, and then their homes. Don't be one of these people.

It comes back to questioning yourself. You have to know you. You have to discover what's at your center, what drives you, what your passion is. If you discover that buying, selling, renovating, or renting property is truly for you, then you have to gird yourself for the journey ahead. You have to do the research. You have to focus on what it is you're trying to achieve. Go ahead and buy a manual if you like. Listen to a CD. Attend a seminar.

Do all this with a discerning eye and a critical mind.

Be prepared for challenges. When you listen to the commercials on the radio and watch the late-night infomercials, they make it all seem so easy. Understand, this is marketing magic at work. It's media-driven consumercelebreality—a small facet, but MDC just the same. The infomercials ply you with images of success, playing to your dreams and deepest desires for immense wealth. Then they tell you it's easy; you can do it to. The truth is you can do it. However, I want you to understand one thing, and it is a truth you should already be aware of.

Nothing worth having, nothing worth doing, nothing worth owning is truly worthwhile without some sweat equity. What is sweat equity? It's your blood, sweat, and tears, your hard work poured vigorously into whatever effort you're trying to make a critical success.

For some it may be easy. For you it may be easy. Some may even use The Secret and wish for something to come to them with ease. I think they mean that clear focus and desire can come with ease. They don't mean the absence of hard work. At least I hope that's not what they're saying.

I'll be honest with you. I believe the Secret was one of the most profitable hustles ever executed. Its success is based on some truth and a whole lot of MDC. I would shake the author's hand for crafting a marketing masterpiece. I would also applaud her for incorporating aspects of positive thinking and advocating clearly knowing what it is you want and reaching for it. This understanding is very powerful. However, I don't advocate wishing for cars and money and expecting it to just come to you. This may work for some. Personally I've never met them, and just sitting and wishing for money to come in my mailbox sure as hell doesn't work for me. I tried it. Nothing happened. In my opinion that's a whole bunch of crap. In fact, the scientific basis described in *The Secret* is pure crap. It sounds good, but it's crap. The pure and unfettered desire for cars, boats, and mansions is entirely contrary to what I believe. However, I can't argue with feeling good and thinking positively. *This* is truly at the core of what I believe. It's my secret.

I'm also a strong advocate of finding what works for you. So if the Secret works for you, more power to you. Personally I do list my objectives, my goals. I do look at them every day and concentrate on making them reality. They are my affirmations. They do have a material component. However, they are truly about me growing as an individual, realizing the wealth I have, and coming into the wealth that will be mine through hard work, planning, and perseverance. More importantly, by being the best me, by becoming an example, I will inspire and motivate others. And when I motivate, I'm always willing to lend a helping hand—to spread blessings and truly give instead of being overly concerned about giving back. Some of us try to look good by bragging about giving back.

People, if you work for it, if you earn it, it's worthwhile. Believe me, you will appreciate your success all the more. You will savor it. You will find favor in the challenge and know that all you've accomplished was truly meant to be. You can feel your very spirit in the building blocks of your effort. It's all yours, and it's a critical success.

Once you do your research, you will find that the information provided in these programs is not for the feint of heart. You must study it. You must learn it. You must be strong and aggressive but positive in your approach. They make it sound easy, but everyone cannot readily dive into this business and be successful. You cannot walk in and structure a complex deal with a seller with no money down and walk away with cash from the table out of the loan two weeks after you read the manual. At least, most of you cannot. If you're like me, average but an aspiring genius, you just can't do it right from the start.

Real estate was very, very nice to me. It will be nice to you if you find it is meant for you. However, you must respect the field. You must learn it. You must be prepared. You must read. You must seek mentors. However, you must avoid the con artist. They are everywhere. Real estate is a cutthroat business. You can lose your life savings, and no one will care. No one will feel sorry for you.

Avoid people who want to form partnerships with you, but use your credit to buy houses with sub-prime loans. Avoid anyone who wants to do more than give you good advice. You'll know the difference. These people are sharks and will eat you alive. They'll take your home, your wife, your children, your dog, your credit, your savings—your very identity if you're not careful and critical. Be discerning. You must ask questions.

Go to a seminar. Don't buy the $1500 informational packet. Don't register for all the overpriced classes and additional training seminars. Take one and use it as a guidepost to gain more information. Conduct your own research.

I'll give you a guarantee. I promise that if real estate is your passion, you will become a self-directed learner and push yourself to succeed in this field. I guarantee you that if you take the time to put together a plan, execute it on at least one property, and find it to your liking, despite the pitfalls and potential losses, you will persevere. You will be happy. You will achieve critical success.

KA-CHING! CASH IN THE POCKET!
SO NOW YOU'RE A DAY TRADER!

People are definitely interested in the stock market. Whereas, once upon a time, it was the playground of the wealthy and connected, the

Internet has given rise to the democratization of the capital markets. With some startup cash, Internet access, and a trading account, anyone can buy and sell stocks, bonds, funds, and even options. Access to an online brokerage allows average Joe Guy to trade stocks for just a few dollars. It's really great! You, me, all of us regular people have access to a veritable playground of financial products.

The capital markets are the home to the world's true financial wealth. Tremendous fortunes are made in this universe of money, as well as lost. It's where people like Warren Buffett and Bill Gates became billionaires, with personal wealth that dwarfs the gross domestic product of some countries.

Think about it.

There are around 300 million people in the United States. If you built an innovative chair that every man, woman, and child in America simply had to have and you sold it for a dollar (this is the incentive to buy) and they all bought one chair, you would have less than half a billion dollars, and that's before taxes and expenses.

Still, it's a helluva lot of money.

However, if you build a company around your product and you decide to take your company public, allowing shares of ownership to be traded in the capital markets, the company could be worth billions of dollars. Your personal share of the company you started could be worth billions of dollars in stocks. Yes, the markets are where incredible amounts of wealth are generated and maintained. Rich people put their money to work in the market. They may have created wealth in the market, but they keep it through prudent (or sometimes not-so-prudent) investments in different sectors of the markets, including real estate.

Today everyone who hears about accessing the stock market from his or her home wants to be creating Bill Gates's type of wealth inside of a month. They have visions of themselves sitting in front of their monitor, trading hundreds of stocks over the course of a day, making tens of thousands of dollars every hour. They have serious delusions of grandeur. Along with this unprecedented access to the financial markets and this alluring grandeur has come a new breed of hustler.

KA-CHING!

Do you want to know a really quick way to go broke and insane? Try day trading. Day trading is a well-known, tried-and-true way to completely lose all your money, as well as your mind. People have gained weight, lost weight, and gained it back again. Day trading can cause all manner of stress-related physiological problems. It's great for building the desire to murder people and commit suicide. Feel free to look it up. So, if you're not so sure about your inner strength and ability to persevere through harsh financial situations, and you're pretty darn sure you want to go insane, give day trading a try. It's sure to satisfy!

Okay, all kidding aside, you can make a substantial amount of money day trading. Many people have. You can also lose everything you have. Many people have. Even for those who want to be active traders as opposed to day traders, the risks can be very high.

A person can make an amazing amount of money in an amazingly short amount of time by just trading in one stock. Still, one has to understand that the opposite also holds true. You can lose an amazing amount of money in an amazing amount of time.

Here's the stock market truth.

If you want to take part in the prosperity that the capital markets provide, then you must participate. However, you must think about how you're going to participate. There are hundreds of systems out there, by hundreds of people. Many of them will tell you they can make you money, if not outright rich. Take a look at what they have to offer. Study them, for free, if you can. I definitely recommend it. You must study what you're about to get into.

Think critically.

Just like the real estate schemes peddled by hucksters, the stock market field is full of hucksters playing to your desires, getting rich off of your ignorance and gullibility. They are taking your money and care nothing for you prosperity. Unfortunately, as long as they aren't committing a crime, it's perfectly legal. It's just business. You must be informed. You must be discerning. You must be critical.

Now, some people are true educators and are worth the money they charge to teach you about the markets. However, no education by any trainer can replace what you will gain by going through the effort of educating yourself. For some people, learning on their own will come naturally. For others, you need a guide, teacher, or mentor. You must question yourself. You must find what you need, focus on it, establish a fundamental plan, and execute it. It all truly starts with finding out if this is a passion for you. You must have some sort of investment in the markets. Everyone should. However, you have to determine if it will be where you experience your critical success.

Personally I think we should all take a crack at trading stocks. Just like in real estate, I don't think you'll ever really know whether or not it's for you unless you give it a try. Some people will do very well and make tons of money. Some will have dismal failures. Here is the best way to go about working the markets:

1. Study! Get books. Read articles. Dive deep into the various financial Web sites. Gather as much information as you can.
2. Discuss in dialogue with others. Learn to talk the markets.
3. Play the markets virtually. You can build a practice portfolio on the Web.
4. Play it for real, but make your stake small. Don't go all-out on your first buy order.
5. Study the markets with a discerning eye.
6. Feel for the trends.
7. Look at your results. Judge them critically.
8. Decide if you're going to continue and move forward.

The markets are all about human emotion. A person with a natural intuitive sense to discern truths from the environment around him may do very well, while a coldly logical and analytical person might possibly fail. No matter what you believe, playing big dollars in the stock market is not for the faint of heart. You can ruin yourself in those violent digital trenches, where wealth and ruin are created in nano-seconds across the digital expanse.

Speak my words. Hear them. Listen. If you decide playing the market requires too much work, find a financial planner. This is important, so I'll say it again. Find a good, reputable financial planner. One person will have a hell of time managing more than ten stocks in a portfolio. And it can turn into a full-time job. Is trading your passion? Will you breathe tick marks? Will you live on the trend line?

If the answer is no, invest, but do it with the help of someone qualified to manage *your* money. I emphasize *your* because every planner is a unique person and therefore different. Find the planner for you and your money.

For those of you who think you can handle some risk but don't want to be full-time day traders or even active traders, here's my recommendation. Study the markets. Study and research the field. Find a financial planner and put most of your investment money in a program. Find, focus on, and establish a fundamental plan, which includes your planner. Determine your level of risk. How much can you afford to work with five thousand, ten thousand, twenty thousand, or five hundred? Know your limit and stick to it. Put most of it into stocks you have picked through careful examination and study. Take the remainder and find the risky stocks you've been looking at closely—the ones you think will be big winners. If it grows, work it. If you lose it all, wait until you earn some more money from your paycheck or whatever and determine if you can get back in. Don't let it become a habit. Don't let it become an addiction. However, the most important thing to remember is to never, ever, ever touch the money you've put in comfortable securities. DO NOT TOUCH THE MONEY YOU PUT IN A PROGRAM WITH THE FINANCIAL PLANNER. That money is sacrosanct. Don't touch it.

THE LOTTERY

Do I really have to put words to paper? Do you need to read the words you know I'm speaking so loudly in my head? Are you one of those people? Do you think you're going to be filthy rich, wealthy, and happy after you win the lottery? Are you one of those people who believes in buying programs that teach you how to win the lottery. If you are, then I have a book for you. It's called 10 *Steps to Winning the Lottery* by D.S. Brown. I recommend you go buy it now.

The rest of you should buy it for fun. It's a good read, in my personal opinion, and you may benefit from it as well. Most of us, the majority, don't need to even bother with this bit of randomness.

We certainly shouldn't be committing large sums of money to the purchase of hundreds of tickets. I've seen someone do this—and miss on all his tickets. It was sad and hilarious at the same time.

The truth about the lottery is that if you don't plan—and I mean really, really plan—then you can't win. If you enjoy the idea of winning and all you do is buy a ticket once a week, then more power to you. Indulge yourself. You're not spending a ton of money, and you may actually win something. However, do not stray beyond your one-ticket-a-week habit. Remember, nothing really worthwhile comes that easy. There's a story out there about a group of people who purposely set out to win the lottery, and they did. Like I said, a good plan. Look 'em up. You will be shocked. And know this: if you win, it won't be easy. Life will become incredibly complicated.

More money, more problems.

ARE YOU A SUCKER?

Some of you have spent hundreds, if not thousands, of dollars on seminars, tapes, DVDs, CDs, and manuals. You've purchased programs you've seen on television in the wee hours of the morning. You've been motivated to call a number you've heard on the radio. You've ordered the free CD, which whetted your appetite and made you want more, dreaming of dollars signs, yachts, sports cars, caviar wishes and champagne dreams.

Few of you, if any, can say you've seen or listened to any of these programs critically. You haven't truly thought critically about what you're good at, where your talents lie, or what you really and truly want to do. You haven't thought about discovering your passion and learning what drives you and how you can use what's real and of substance in your spirit to drive the generation of personal wealth.

Some of you would happily be led to the doorway of your dreams and merrily step through to discover a vast pool of emptiness bordered by other doors to more empty pools, each door demanding an entrance fee. You would pay. You would walk through. You would smile. And then you would pay again. You would keep thinking, *the next one. Yeah, the next one, this one. This is for real!* You would spend $1,400 for a packet of information on how to get rich. You would happily invest $50,000, your entire savings, in some kind of marketing scheme for a product you really haven't studied worth a damn. You would hope to fly on a hope and prayer and fall disastrously on your face, ripping, tearing and rolling soundly over on your ass, ruining every part of your body, as someone else smiled last and smiled best. Well, of course they would smile. They're getting rich!

Is this you? Am I describing you? Have you ever fallen victim? Many of you have at one time or another. Do some of you remember *Friends helping Friends*? It was a classic pyramid scheme in which people would be invited to put in up to $2,000 when they entered the bottom of the pyramid, and collect more than $12,000 when they cash out at the top. All you had to do was recruit others. However, don't get stuck at the bottom or in the middle. Do you know what this makes you? Do you know what people call you? I know! I was just like you, though I never went overboard. Uh, and well, I never got caught at the bottom of the pyramid.

If this is you, then you're a ...

Yes, that's correct. You're a sucker. If you learn one thing from all that I've written, learn to not be a sucker. This means you have to be discerning. This means you have to question. This means you have to be critical. Commit to never again being a victim.

Recognize the lies and acknowledge the truth. What is the truth? The truth is that in America, if you can figure out a way to generate wealth and it's not illegal, then you're welcome to it. The people who put these programs and schemes together are simply realizing their own American dream. They've clearly figured out their passion or what drives them. They know how to sell. This is what they're good at, and they revel in it. They're walking talking MDC. They convince you that they're going to make you rich, and you believe them.

Understand, you can't knock them for this, not if it's legal. They're simply trying to get paid. They want to generate wealth, just like you. Remember, most of these people are getting wealthy from your purchase of their intellectual property (manual, CDs, and tapes). Make no mistake; right now I'm working on doing something similar. However, look at what I'm attempting to do with a discerning eye. Be critical of me.

I'm a capitalist. It's not a bad word. I'm an entrepreneur. People really seem to like this word. I'm a social liberal and a fiscal conservative. I'm critical of myself and others. This is me. You don't have to be like me. You have to figure out how to be you and generate your success. David Hannum said there's a sucker born every minute. Listen, people. Listen for the sounds of the swindler. When you hear them, smile, turn, and walk away, shaking your head at their shame. Don't be a sucker.

Know the barriers to critical success:

Lack of critical thinking skills
Media-driven Consumercelebreality
Willful assumption of debt
GET-RICH-QUICK SCHEMES!

We will achieve critical success through critical thinking. We will be discerning. We will question. We see and hear the affects of media-driven consumercelebreality We recognize it and will not succumb to it. We can sidestep the willful assumption of debt. We avoid the get-rich-quick schemes, as they are nothing more than traps for suckers. We are not suckers.

Tip Table For Knowing When Someone Is Trying to Treat You Like a Sucker

IF	THEN
1. You've been invited to THE MOST IMPORTANT SEMINAR you'll ever attend on getting RICH!	⇨ Run away. It's crap!
2. Several big-name individuals will be in attendance to help you realize your dream of getting rich!	⇨ Run away. It's crap!
3. The founders of the company couldn't make it to the seminar, but the person speaking can testify to how much money you'll make because he/she is making money hand over fist, and they show slides of the founders' Hummers, yachts, and mansions.	⇨ Run away quickly. It's total crap!

4. You're at the seminar and
    they're perfectly willing
    to help you become a real
    estate tycoon, media mogul,
    or stock market wizard for
    the low, low price of *up to a
    thousand* or so dollars.

    ⇨ Frown! Shake your head,
    turn, and run away fast.
    It's total crap!

5. You sit through half the
    seminar and you never learn
    how it is you're going to
    make money. All you hear is
    that you'll be able to make
    hundreds of thousands of
    dollars in very little time.
    Then you see testimonials of
    successful people making up
    to thirty thousand dollars a
    week.

    ⇨ You're kidding, right?
    ⇨ Please, please run away.
    It's total crap!

6. Your friend invites you to
    the seminar and explains
    that you can come into
    the organization under
    him and you'll both make
    money together, and in the
    meantime he tries to sell you
    a phone card.

    ⇨ Smile and tell him
    sincerely he should look
    for a sucker elsewhere.
    ⇨ Then, of course, run. It's
    total crap!

CHAPTER 7
THE 10 POINT PLAN

We've identified the barriers to critical success. We know what they are. As time passes, you will become more proficient at identifying MDC. You will become stronger and resist the willful assumption of debt. You will smile as you listen to the people attempting to lure you in with their get-rich-quick schemes. You will listen to them carefully, wary of any nuggets of truth you can exploit to your own benefit. Most importantly, you will embrace the way of the critical thinker.

For some of you, this is really all you'll need. Some of you know what it is you want to do. The idea is already in your head. You now have a poem that you can read every day to reinforce your attitude. As you drive toward utilizing your passion to build personal wealth, you will seek other opportunities to bolster your position, to help you along on your journey, and allow you some cushion just in case things don't work out on the first, second, or third try. However, you will remain critical, discerning, and positive. You are shining, and nothing can take that away.

People who are ready to execute a plan on their passion usually have been blessed in understanding the critical need to establish a financial base, or what we can call a financial foundation. They inherently understand F-PEC, Fundamental Personal Economic Control. They strive to maintain control over their finances, cushioning themselves from the impact of external events such as rising gas prices or even the loss of a job. They have the right insurance. They have three months' income in savings in case of a job loss. They maintain a budget. They know the inflows and outflows of money from their household. They have spent most of their lives being responsible with their finances. They haven't fallen victim to the barriers. They have always been aware of them on some level, but because they weren't easy prey, they didn't take the time to consider it. They knew it was stupid to build up a load of debt on their one or two credit cards. They just didn't do it.

For the rest of us? Spoons.

Those of us who didn't grow up knowing how to be financially responsible, who for whatever reason were victims of MDC from an early age, have need of a plan; if not a plan, at least a guide to help us navigate our way around and through the barriers to critical success. We need something that will help us establish F-PEC. We need something that will aid us in building our financial foundation. Those of us who are ready know that once we've established this foundation, we can pursue critical success in earnest, with all the heart and drive we can muster. However, we know we must move forward one step at a time. We know we need to think and develop a plan.

Following is the process that is at the core of critical success: The "2 rules of 3." By utilizing this plan, you will learn to actively address your personal financial situation. You will learn to think critically about who you are and what you truly want to accomplish. As you work through each step and discover more about who you are and what you want to do and be, you will be making a conscious decision. With each step forward, you are working toward critical success. You are deciding to succeed.

Critical Success: The 10-Point Plan!

1) **Step 1: Stop and Think**
Where do you stand? Are you thinking *critically* about your financial situation? Are you hanging on to debt? Are you thinking *critically* about your debt? Are you jumping into lotteries, get-rich-quick schemes, and investments without thinking? Are you even thinking about what you really want to do with your life?

2) **Step 2: Know The Painful Truth**
Are you are a walking catastrophe, a whale of debt? You must establish F-PEC: Fundamental Personal Economic Control. (credit and debt planning).

3) **Step 3: Look in the Mirror and Paint the Picture**
Understand your financial situation in total, and if you are in trouble, acknowledge this fact. Know that if you continue along the same path, you will never achieve your objectives, let alone comfort in your old age. You will have pain. You will suffer. You could very well die from stress. You must see yourself and paint your picture.

4) **Step 4: Isolate (Find and Identify) the Flaws**
Now that you understand the picture of you, isolate the things that need to change. List what needs work, what's broken in your life. This is the start of using the tool.

5) **Step 5: Use the Tool: 3FE**
You are solution-seeking. 3FE is a tool for simple thinking. Find, Focus, and establish the Fundamentals, and Execute. Applying it is motivating, and seeing its results is empowering. Use the tool to build a plan for wealth and comfort.

6) **Step 6: Understand the 3 Principles of Prosperity (3PoP)**
Do everything necessary to make sure you're happy, satisfied, and comfortable. Work on having real estate. Work on investing in the capital markets. Work on opening a business. Detail your steps and formulate your plan.

7)   **Step 7: Know the Clear Discipline of Effective Execution**
Discipline. The word sounds as hard as it is. Few of us are lucky. The rest think, plan, and work very hard in order to succeed. You must have the discipline required to see it through. It is a contest with yourself, and you must be determined not to fail.

8)   **Step 8: Why Do We Fall? So We Can Get Back Up Again!**
Acknowledge the possibility of failure. Acknowledge the times when we don't want to move forward, the times when we want to quit. Then straighten up your attitude, know the *secret that works for you*, and be positive. Pick yourself up and try again.

9)   **Step 9: Follow the Real Yellow Brick Road**
Step nine is simply a state of mind. The yellow brick road is real, and if you're doing the right things, you will be walking on it. The road may be long and winding, but you can get to the end. It will be different for each of us, giving us joy and pain to suit who we are and our life experiences.

10) **Step 10: Walk into the Clear**
With your bills paid and some financial freedom, you have the room to truly consider 3PoP. What is your future going to look like? Will you open a franchise? Will you build an entertainment complex, a mixed-use community? What can you do with your savings and your new free time? What will you do?

So what are you going to do?

Are you now like I once was? Do you have to start at square one and clean up you life? Do you have to build a solid financial framework where none existed? Do you feel your purpose and see your objective, but know that you are blocked by the barriers? Do you see your critical success? Do you know it? Are you ready to claim it?

What are you going to do?

Would you like to open a franchise? Then you will need a solid foundation. You will need to know yourself and be able to smash through the barriers. You will need to be mentally prepared to do your research and financially able to support the effort. The educational imperative is a must. It will facilitate the building of your foundation and propel you toward success. When planning on starting some other kind of business, the same applies, no matter what it is you want to do. Do you have plans to invent something and sell it? Again, the same applies. So are you ready? The first thing you have to do, if you're fully ready to make a commitment to achieving critical success, is *stop and think.*

There are programs out there that guarantee you the chance to not only make money; they promise they will make you rich. Now, please understand that the critical success program is all about achieving success. It's about you finding what drives you, what makes you feel happy, what quantifies your success, and how in the process you can become quite wealthy.

Remember, the word *rich*, as we commonly understand it, is simply not what everyone needs. Being rich does not necessarily mean having money. Wealth does not mean you're flush with cash. By going through this program, it is my sincere hope that you do become monetarily wealthy, at least to the point that cash is not a major concern. This is the goal we should all aspire to. I want you to be rich in life, love, and happiness. I want your wealth to be quantified in hundreds of thousands of dollars in cash and millions in investments, as well as indescribable life experiences and love shared between you, your children, your extended family, and your friends.

The critical success program emphasizes critical thinking. It is a necessary skill that you must develop in order to achieve success. You must become the best individual you can be, and in order to do this, you must be able to make sound decisions. You must be able to stop and think.

At the heart of the critical success program is the "10 Point Plan. The plan is all about utilizing critical thinking skills. Of course, it is centered around your financial situation and discovering what you can do to build personal wealth and have a truly rich life. However, by embarking on this journey of discovery, along the way you should discover that which drives you, that which is your true passion, that which you love to do, and hopefully that which will allow you to attain financial freedom and enjoy life without the worries of bills being paid, children going to college, and who will take care of you when you retire. You will have enough cash set aside in programs so that you can take care of yourself.

The details of the 10-Point Plan start in the next chapter. By following the plan and utilizing the 2 Rules of 3, you will discover your personal truth. You will come to know you, and what you can, and should achieve. You will define the plan that truly works for you. You make right, what is wrong and achieve all you that you can with what you have been given.

However, before proceeding to the next chapter, I want you to make sure you have a loose-leaf notebook. I also want you to have several sheets of loose-leaf paper. If you don't have this, go out and purchase it from your local drugstore, Staples, or Office Depot. Why am I asking you to have this material? All of the information you will accumulate over the course of the 10 Steps will represent the story of you and how you achieved critical success. At the end of the process, I want you to take all that information and rewrite it. Reorganize it. Place it in the notebook. What you will have is the story of your personal journey toward critical success. It will become:

The _____ *(your name here)* 10-Step Book For Critical Success.

Finally, if you're willing, I would like you to share your story with me personally. Who knows. You may win something.

CHAPTER 8
STEP 1: STOP
AND THINK

STOP!

Stop right now and consider your situation. Where are you? What are you doing? Why are you doing what you do? How are you doing what you do, and can you not do better? If so, when will you start? Who are you?

Stop and think. Consider. Question. Ask yourself, *who am I?* Do you truly know? Have you ever really taken the time to consider this question? I ask it again: do you know who you are? Cognition, my friends. Thinking is incredibly important.

Where do you stand? Are you thinking critically about your future? Are you thinking *critically* about your current financial situation? Have you built a foundation? Are you beset by the barriers? Are you hanging on to debt? Are you thinking *critically* about your debt? Are you jumping into get-rich-quick schemes and investments without thinking? Are you even thinking about what you really want to do with your life? You! Yes, you! Right now.

STOP AND THINK!

Thinking. The word sounds simple. It easily rolls off the tongue. We all take thinking for granted. And that's fair. After all, we are always thinking. What we must consider is how well we think. Truly nothing is more important. Your ability to think is even more powerful when coupled with your innate ability of self-awareness. You know who you are, but really, do you know who you are? Do you truly think beyond the rudimentary? As human beings, we don't think enough. We don't stop and consider what's going on around us. The majority of us question nothing. Like one of my favorite songs from my youth says, "It's like that, and that's the way it is!" It sounds good, but we can't go through life being so accepting. We can't be automatons.

Think about it. Can life be like what a young John Conner said in the movie *Terminator 2*: *There is no fate, but what we make.*

How's that for being young and assaulted by MDC.

Step one is asking you to change the way you approach life. It's asking you to become the kind of person I've been asking you to be all along, a critical thinker. Only when utilizing your mind can you experience growth. You must view your cognitive ability like you do an exercise program. The more you exercise, the more able you become. The same applies for your mind. If you exercise it, it will become more efficient. You must read. You must read. You must engage in dialogue. You must communicate. You must ponder, question, answer, find, focus, establish a fundamental plan, and execute.

I think most of you will freely admit that if we did think more often than we act, we would all be far better off. We frequently act on impulse, be it buying a box of doughnuts on a whim or driving by a car dealership for six days and on the seventh day stopping and buying that brand spanking new, candy-paint red convertible. Oh, the agony of a new $590 a month car note—and it's a lease. Oh, the agony. Some of you even entertain the idea of an $850 car note. What in the world could you possibly be thinking? And I personally know a person who carried a note on an expensive designer watch. PEOPLE, THE MAN HAD A MONTHLY PAYMENT ON A WATCH! This displays a fundamental lack of critical thinking, and by leveraging your future earnings, which could be applied to your fundamental plan for critical success, you are being slapped soundly into the ground by the first barrier. Your lack of critical thinking is keeping you mired in debt, smashing you into the earth, threatening to bury you so deep that you might not be able crawl out for years, if ever, if you don't change the way you think. Let's ask some simple questions:

Are you happy?
Do you have a lot of debt?
Do you have a lot of credit card debt?
(We have to make the distinction.)
Is your car really worth the amount you pay on it every month?
Is your house pretty, large, and very, very expensive?
Honestly, can you afford your large, pretty house?
Do you sleep well at night?

I want you to write the questions down on paper and look at them. This will comprise the first section of your ten-step book for critical success. Think about these questions. Don't answer them just yet. I want you to mull them over in your head. As the truth bubbles to the top of your mind or tries to come screaming out of your mouth, push it back down and think about it little more.

This will be a quick process for some of you. You already know the truth. You have been close to taking action. You don't have a good plan. However, you know you have to do something. Some of you know you're in trouble but have no idea how to get yourselves out. You want help, but you continue to live your lives of fake floss and flash. You want success, but the iron anchor of debt is holding you back.

All of this is okay—if you wrote down the questions. Then you're well on your way.

By simply doing step one, stopping and thinking, you're being courageous. You're taking the time to think about who you are and what you've been doing. This introspection is not something we often do. As modern people, we tend to avoid the problems we face, if we can, because ignoring them feels so much better. This is a lie that we tell ourselves, and it is only fleeting. The lie feels good only on the surface and only for so long.

Do you say the following things to solidify the lie?

But I need a luxury car. What will people think?
My club membership is very important! It's a must-have!
If I don't own the best clothes, I won't look professional at work.
I simply must eat out at least twice a week—and be seen.
I have an image, a reputation, to maintain.

Do you live in a mini-mansion filled with plasma screens and have a manicured lawn, painful utility bills, and manic neighbors living on the edge of depression? Do you want to change? *I have an image, a reputation, to maintain.* This statement is very important to the many of you who crave critical success. You think it's part of your success when nothing could be further from the truth. In fact, the superficial nature of this statement denies you access to true success. It is a derivation of the MDC disease. You're living a commercial life that is bound to break your back, literally. You're so busy thinking about what others think that you spend far too little time thinking about yourself, discovering yourself, and learning why you matter, what your passion is, and what your true contribution should be in this world.

There are many people out there who manage to look quite professional though they shop at outlet stores. Are you going to let your clothes dictate your success? I'll tell you now; there is a vast difference between looking the part and living the part. If you're living it and you can afford to waste a little money, then by all means do it. Enjoy yourself. However, do not let your desire to look fabulous prevent **you** from actually being fabulous.

Think **about** it.

Some of you are certain you're ready to achieve critical success. You haven't completed your foundation. Your finances aren't fully in order, but you feel you should go for it. You can make it. How? You're convinced that if you join a certain organization, read its manual, and follow its program, you'll be rich. Yes, they have a plan for you, and you're ready to follow it all the way to champagne wishes and caviar dreams.

Are you concerned about your retirement? Call now to receive your FREE business evaluation kit. There is immediate income potential if you get started in one of our turnkey programs. You can make money from the comfort of your own home.

This is a world of high-energy costs and gasoline prices that bite a shark-sized hole out of your wallet. Please allow me to show you how to get rich and conserve energy at the same time. By dropping a simple additive in your fuel tank every day, you can extend the mileage on you car by as much as 50 percent.

People, we've gone over all this before.

In the gasoline additive example, an already wealthy and successful individual invested $500,000 into a gas-additive scheme. He lost all his money. Thankfully the authorities were successful in locating the criminal that was sponsoring the scheme and put him behind bars. He won't be conning anyone else for quite some time.

An additive in fuel that can extend your car's mileage by 50 percent? Come on, people! Do you know how revolutionary that would be? Do you really know how many billions of dollars would be on the line for something like this? Do you really think the person or organization that develops such a thing would market through a seminar at your local hotel and ship the stuff to you by mail so you can sell it to your friends and family? Do you really think they would share all those billions with you when they can sell the stuff themselves and make a killing?

Think about it.

As I said before, David Hannum surely did put it very well: "there's a sucker born every minute." Don't be a sucker.

People want to make money. They go through their day-to-day routine and are steady on the *grind!* They need hope. They're reaching for a brighter future. They are eagerly looking for an opportunity. They run smack-dab headfirst into an opportunist. These people who want wealth (or want to grow their wealth) are regular folks. Some of them are spoons. However, others are quite sharp knives that act like spoons—knoons (knives, forks, and spoons). A special on *20/20* showed this fact quite clearly. Wealthy individuals looking for investments were getting fleeced by industrious criminal Nigerians. It was amazing. They were being swindled again and again and again. Personally I was dumbfounded. These were hard-working individuals who had earned large amounts of money creating a great deal of wealth. They were seemingly intelligent people being hoodwinked time and again. It was stupendously stupid, just amazing.

Say it aloud and listen: *it's MDC.* That is truly what it is. You simply have to be thinking critically so you can recognize it. The purveyors of these enterprises, both legal and illegal, are charismatic and bright. You and I are starving for the good life, and these people tell us they can provide it. Because we aren't thinking, we listen and we believe, to our eventual detriment.

I know it's hard. Strong desire and sincere hope can erode your ability to think clearly, let alone critically. However, you cannot—must not—falter. Investigate every opportunity. Look it up on the Internet. Call Clark Howard and ask for his advice. Apply the power of 3FE. Do whatever you must to peel back the covers and discern the complications, the complexities, and in some cases the unfortunate truth.

Again, understand clearly: if someone has a method of making millions, why would they share it with you thousands? Think critically, my friends. If someone is getting paid to tell you how to get rich, how do you think they got rich? It certainly wasn't selling pills, stocks, or real estate. What in the world do you think I'm doing by having you read this book? *Well, that's what I'm trying to do.*

Stop!

Think!

Understand the barriers. What are they?

A total lack of critical thinking skills
Infection by MDC (Media-Driven Consumercelebreality)
The willful assumption of debt
Participating in get-rich-quick schemes

I'm not asking you to become a critical thinking expert. I am demanding that you try. As you journey down the critical thinker's road, if you don't eventually become an expert, you will still become a critical thinker along the way. I'm not asking you to become a questioning pest. However, I am demanding that you still question everything. I do understand the pain that sometimes accompanies thinking and questioning. I know many of you don't want to think about what's going on around you, what's happening to you, because it is so very painful. I know many of you prefer to run from your pain, to hide from it. I know that many of you are afraid of thinking about your lives. However, you cannot succumb. You cannot give in to despair. You need to stop and think about your situation.

Stop! Right now!

Think! Right now!

YOU HAVE TO STOP AND THINK! IT IS THE FIRST STEP ON THE ROAD TO CRITICAL SUCCESS!

CHAPTER 9
STEP 2: KNOW THE
PAINFUL TRUTH

At the end of the previous chapter, we were talking about running away from pain. We discussed the first step on the path to critical success. I emphasized the need for us—all of us, wealthy or not—to stop and think. For those of us infected by MDC, the act of stopping and thinking will usually lead to grappling with pain.

There was a commercial being utilized by a certain bank as part of their MDC campaign. It was obviously part of their marketing plans to generate additional revenue for their home mortgage business. I can't knock them for trying to make an honest buck. Their commercial played off of our desire to be free of MDC. For those of us suffering through the deep pain of MDC, we needed the type of message they were providing. We needed to know that someone understood us and was ready and willing to lend a hand. However, in order to escape the ravages of MDC, we needed a little bit more than a commercial with a guy smiling as though he was crying at the same time. "I'm in debt up to my eyeballs," he cried. "Will somebody help me?"

Now, do you think it's the bank that he really needs?

The bank may be part of his solution, but he needs to look to himself and his family to correct his situation. He needs to eliminate his debt and start working on building wealth. Simply said but not so simply done.

Let's study this man for a moment. His name is Stanley Johnson. He's got a great family, wife, and three kids. He stays in a beautiful four-bedroom house with an in-ground pool in a great community. He's got a brand new SUV. He even belongs to the local golf club. In the commercial Stanley asks the pivotal question, "How do I do it?" And of course, the response is what I've stated previously. He's in debt up to his eyeballs, and it is not pretty. He tells us he can barely pay his finance shares. You can plainly see the stress under his strained smile.

Stanley knows he's in trouble. He knows he's on the brink. He's pretending on the outside, but on the inside, he's in turmoil. He needs to know the painful truth both inside and out. He needs to accept his situation and come up with a plan to address it.

What applies to Stanley applies to us all. Are you a walking catastrophe? Are you a whale of debt? Do you want to cry in the dark watches of the night, terrified that the world will discover that you're actually broke; you're about to go into bankruptcy and lose your new car, your four-bedroom house with the pool, and your golf club membership? Or are you about to get kicked out of your apartment and lose your car and what little bit of respect you had? Each of us must learn to establish F-PEC. F-PEC is fundamental personal economic control.

Fundamental: Serving as or being an essential part of a foundation or basis. Of great significance or entailing major change.

Personal: Of or relating to a particular person; private.

Economic: Pertaining to the production, distribution, and use of income, wealth, and commodities.

Control: To exercise authoritative or dominating influence over; direct. To hold in restraint; check.

Each of us needs to build a foundation that pertains to us personally and allows us to exercise influence and restraint over the distribution of our income. We need debt planning. We need budgets. We need assistance where it can be provided. We need to change our mindset. We need to start considering ourselves and our future. We need to cure ourselves of MDC, stop thinking about what others think, and start thinking about ourselves and our posterity. Yes, that's right: your children, your descendants. We must each consider what we will leave behind. This is F-PEC.

WHO ARE YOU?

WHAT CAN YOU DO?

WHAT WILL BE YOUR CONTRIBUTION?

WHAT WILL YOU LEAVE TO THOSE WHO COME AFTER YOU?

Do you want prosperity for you and your posterity? If this is what you want—if you truly want to build wealth, and it's not just something you like to say to your friends in the afternoon after lunch, as a dream of something that's going to happen in a few years after you get over the hump—then you must acknowledge the *painful truth*!

You are a whale of debt! It is time for you to correct the situation. It is time for *you* to establish F-PEC.

Many of us live our lives in the midst of financial ruin or right on the very edge. We go through life generating ever-increasing amounts of debt, collecting more and more stuff, marginalizing our futures and our children's futures. This has to stop. We have to start thinking.

We have to learn through introspection. We have to teach ourselves. We have to come to grips with our inner desires. We have to dispel the affects of MDC and concentrate on our needs first. We have to establish our foundation and grow wealth the old fashioned way. If we have ideas and plan, when opportunity comes knocking, we will be prepared.

We must avoid the schemes. We cannot reach for *lifestyles of the rich and famous* by way of lottery tickets, flickering stock screens, or the promise of flipping house after house for cash in an imagined real estate empire that spans the city. We cannot rely on pills in our gas tanks.

Take a good, hard look at yourself. Acknowledge the pain of your financial situation. Accept it. Own it like you never have before. Know that it's a disaster. Know the truth. Know that it can and will destroy your finances, your family, and your very life if you let it. Stop hiding from it. Stop disguising it behind a thin veil of pretend wealth. Look at it. Lay claim to this fiction that is your life. Own it. If the truth as that you have almost $75,000 in credit card debt, then acknowledge this as the truth. Own it. Think critically about it, and make a commitment to change your situation. Commit to making it better. Commit to establishing F-PEC. Fundamental personal economic control will be yours.

Breathe easy.

In your 10 step book for critical success, make a bold statement about your pain. Write down what it is. Write down how it makes you feel. If you cried, write the story of your cry. If you screamed, write the tale of your screaming. What is your pain? Are you truly ready? Do you accept it? If you're ready and accept it, then write it down. Write your statement of strength and willingness to move forward. Write your affirmation.

It's scary, but take heart in the fact that you've accepted reality. You're ready to move on. You know the awful truth. However, you are ready and willing to correct it. You're thinking critically. You're prepared to look even closer at yourself and fix what's broken. You're ready to discover who you are, or rather who you have been. You're on the road to building your foundation and becoming someone else. You're on your way to freeing yourself from MDC. You're ready to look in the mirror and paint your picture.

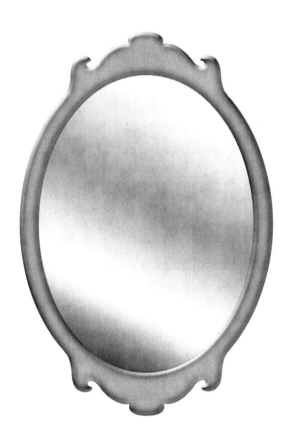

CHAPTER 10
STEP 3: LOOK IN
THE MIRROR AND
PAINT THE PICTURE

Once you've acknowledged the painful truth, it's time to look at yourself critically and commit the awful truth to paper. That's right. We're really getting into it now. Write it all down as part of your ten-step book for critical success. You might even consider doing it in red ink for added emphasis. You must look in the mirror and paint the picture of you. As an individual, examine yourself critically. What have you done in your life? How are the barriers preventing you from achieving critical success? Let's go back to the example of Stanley Johnson.

We've discussed the painful truth—that you may be a walking whale of debt, that you're a victim of MDC with no F-PEC, that if you continue along the same lines you will never achieve your objectives. You will have pain. You will suffer. You could eventually even die a sad and awful death brought on by stress.

Paint your picture.

Write it down. Write it all down. This step is designed to move your mind, mirror, and picture. Look at yourself and write it all down. This step is the jumping-off point to decisive action. By going through the exercise of detailing the various aspects of your life, you're moving yourself forward in a direction that will lead to freedom from MDC and eventual critical success.

I understand this is hard. Believe me, you are not alone. Understand, I didn't just sit here one day and divine all of this out of the crack of my backside. Know that I have lived this journey. In an attempt to get rich quickly, then get rich at a medium pace, then get rich slowly by thinking critically, I discerned these steps. They manifested from action. I was the debt-ridden whale. I had to look at my ugly-ass self and figure out I was screwing up my future. I had to come to realize that I was being poisoned by MDC and if I didn't straighten up my situation, I might die from stress, broke and homeless. Yes, it was getting that bad. I owe a great deal of my salvation to my wife. She helped me get back on track. Her actions are a testament to the fact that sometimes you need help. If you need help, don't hesitate to ask for it. Just think critically about who you ask. I suggest the Consumer Credit Counseling Services, but that's just me. (I've been there too.) I'm actually moving ahead of myself. We'll get to that step later. For now let's focus on your painted (written) picture.

Understand that only you can make this happen. Only you can change the path you're on and move toward that golden road leading to critical success. It's entirely up to you. No amount of information I give you or direction I can provide will give you what you need unless you're ready to receive it, unless you've had enough and you're ready to shirk off the lunacy of MDC and the spoonishness of your cultivated desire for all the shiny things or big-wheeled things for all the floss and flash, bling and blast.

Hear my voice in your head as if it was coming from a megaphone. Listen, we're going to make this quite simple. It's time to tell you how to paint this picture with words. It doesn't have to be complicated. It won't be a Renoir (go look him up, if necessary).

Here's what I want you to do. Take a pen or pencil and a piece of paper. Gather all your bills together. This step is all about getting a firm understanding of your financial picture. If you go to Consumer Credit Counseling Services, they'll do this part for you. It's really great, and scary, but uplifting when you know you—I'm getting ahead of myself, again. I apologize. I'm just getting really excited right now as I type this, with the thought that you—yes you, reading these words—are taking this seriously and embarking on a journey of personal healing. I can't tell you what a lift I get out of it. So, you see, helping you is symbiotic for me. I get something out of it too. I get that feel-good feeling, which is as good as gold, in some instances.

Back to pen or pencil and paper.

I want you to start by writing down how much money you and your family earn in a week, in a month, and in a year. On another piece of paper I want you to write down how much money you spend on a daily basis. I want you to think of everything: sodas, chewing gum, sandwiches for lunch, breath mints, whatever. I want you to add up these *extraneous* expenses. I want you to think critically about this. If necessary, err on the side of indulgence; add a few extra dollars for those things you're not thinking about. Add this figure up for the week, the month, and then the year. What we're doing here is building your basis of crap expenses, the things you burn your change on, which really adds up to dollars flying out of your pocket.

Get another sheet of paper. Write down all the bills you pay on a monthly basis. Don't miss a detail. Write them all down, mortgage or rent, electricity, gas, water, everything. You need to understand clearly how much money you're bringing in, the first sheet with you earnings, and how much you're spending, the sheet with the extraneous expenses. You need all the details.

Listen, going forward, I want you to keep all your receipts and bills and write down your expenses on a daily basis. You need to be keeping a running record of what you're spending your money on every day. This is a critical component of your budget.

YES, I SAID BUDGET. YOU'RE GOING TO HAVE A BUDGET. Too many people don't have a budget. They don't compare their income against their expenditures, and it's CRAZY! They don't think about how much they spend in comparison to how much they make. They just don't. It's one of the most horrendous symptoms of media-driven Consumercelebreality. These people see bills coming in every day and simply rack 'em and stack 'em. They pay whenever they can, whatever they can. People, this is highly spoonish and is no way to go through life.

Okay, here comes a spike in the pain.

Take out another piece of paper, clean and pristine. Get your writing instrument ready. We're going to do a bit of self-analysis. Put your critical thinking caps on tight, and ask the all-important question: *how did you get to this point?*

Did you buy too much jewelry and a $75,000 Mercedes Benz, when you and your spouse earn only $75,000 a year? Was it your spouse? Or was it both of you together, two spoons in a blanket, burning through cash, trying to live the fabulously stupid fabulous life you see on TV at the rate of fabulocity? I love Kimora Lee Simmons. You can't be her. There's only one, and she's an original!

What habits have you picked up over the years? Where do you see your money going without fail? Is it a necessary habit? Be honest with yourself. Think about it. Don't avoid it. Face it with courage. You know what you did. You know what you're doing. How did you become a walking catastrophe, a whale of debt? Write it all down, every ugly detail.

After you're written it all down, read it aloud. That's right, READ IT OUT LOUD! Let it sink in. Look at all you're written down, at the papers you've covered. You have inflow and outflows of cash. You have extraneous expenses. You have bills. You have an explanation as to why you're at this point in life. You have a picture. It's ugly, but it's beautiful at the same time. Now, you can see it all. You can speak to it aloud. Now, you have one more step to complete this picture of you and your situation.

Think critically about your future.

This is where the rubber hits the road, people. It's gets no more real than this. Imagine what next year is going to be like for you, for your family. Imagine what your life will be like five years from now if you continue down the same path. Think about ten years from now, twenty years from now. What about retirement?

Are you thinking about it? If you are, good. Now write it down. How do you do this? You can't account for all the factors, but the picture you've painted will allow us to extrapolate (look it up) your future for you. I'm going to continue to KISS (keep it simple, stupid) this analysis. We won't get complicated. Just do the following:

1. Add up how much you're saving a year (the truth, for you zero people).
2. Add up how much you're earning from wages, salary, etc., in a year.
3. Add up how much you're spending in a year (reference your written picture).
4. Add your savings and your earnings.
5. Subtract your spending from the sum of your savings and your earnings.
6. Do this for five, ten, twenty, and thirty years.
7. Look at the final number. Just look at it.

Is your final number a positive number. Is it small or large? Is it a negative number? Do you have a negative number after thirty years of employment? How far in the negative is the number? This should be very illuminating, especially for you MDC victims. Of course, as I said, this is not a very complicated process, and it does not take into account a myriad number of life variables, rises in income, inflation, financial windfalls, and/or disasters. Life happens to all of us. However, it does give you a basis, a foundation to work with, completing a picture that can be quite scary. People, a negative number is a tragedy. How will you live in retirement? People, this is serious! We must move from being a spending society back to a saving society. Look at your picture. Just look at it.

You want critical success. You know you could die from the stress of living a life in constant debt, owing others, never being able to pursue your desires to achieve the success you deserve, to know the sheer joy of financial freedom. Critical success is all about discerning reality from fantasy and achieving your full potential through concerted effort, strong commitment, passion, and faith. If you want it, you must thirst for it. You must burn for it.

There is no room for spoons. There is no room for those who wallow in MDC and choose laziness and entitlement over hard work and the battle to beat down adversity. There is strength and wisdom in the conquest of adversity. Know that the painful and bleak picture you've created is not a permanent thing. The very act of acknowledging and working through the issues is an incredibly powerful step forward. Take heart in the fact that you are well on your way. You are on the cusp of true planning, which means you will get to your very own promised plan. You're ready for the next step. For you, sunshine and happy days could be just around the corner.

CHAPTER 11
STEP 4: ISOLATE
(FIND AND IDENTIFY)
THE FLAWS

Ladies and gentleman, we are going with GAS!

We've got forward momentum, and let me tell you, we are not stopping. In fact, we are picking up speed. We are critical thinkers putting together plans that are solution-oriented, motivating, and empowering. We are, *as they so often say,* doing the damn thang!

You have acknowledged the painful truth. You are fully aware of your picture. Why? Because, you painted it. In fact, while you were so busy painting, you took the time to document how you got here, to this point, rich and overflowing with the poison of MDC. However, it no longer matters. You are prepared. You are ready. You're going with gas.

What do we do now?

We move on to step four. We take a good look at the picture we've painted and start to isolate those things that are truly causing us problems. We identify those things that we're doing that are really dragging us down. It's time to pick out the hard parts, the bad parts, the cold curves of black ice that cause you to slip lower and lower, down into the ravine of despair.

We focus our eyes on those things that are hopeless, drowning happy byways to the land of ignorance and bliss, where no one experiences critical success and spoon culture reigns supreme. It's a place where you come to believe fervently in the Entitlement Nation, where someone, everyone, owes you something, not the other way around, and you rationalize that the people you owe shouldn't expect so much from you. What are they, stupid? You come to believe in the indisputable, immutable right to accumulate destructive debt. This is a land where, at a moment's notice, a late-night infomercial stomps soundly on critical thinking, and you suddenly believe you'll be a millionaire in a matter of months. You buy manuals on real estate and stock options. You investigate flipping houses for 50 percent profit and rental homes that generate 30 percent free cash flow every month. You have an honest and sincere belief that by playing the state lottery diligently every week, you—just you, especially you—have a very good chance of winning.

Yes, we are isolating the things in your life that promote this mode of thought. We're about excising this cancer from your mind and body. We're about isolating them, and blasting them with a strong fortified dose of true rationality and critical thinking. We are about destroying the spoonishness in our lives, eliminating the stupidity of MDC, and stepping forward into a new land of clear thought and planned action.

Grab your pen and paper.

I need you to look at the picture of yourself, those disparate pieces of paper that build the basic financial picture of your life. Look at it with a very critical, discerning eye. Glance over the statement about how you got to this point. Take the pen and start writing down what needs work, what's broken in your life, what things are generating those mountains of debt. What things are contributing to the barriers and preventing you from working toward critical success?

You'll notice that the entire first portion of the 10 Point Plan is an exercise it utilizing the *Find* function of 3FE. We are actively finding those things in our lives that require work. You're looking at your picture and writing down the flaws. You're isolating them and putting them on paper with your own hand, making them more solid, more real—something you can see, share, and address. When discussing them with your family or the close personal friends or advisors you're confiding in to help you through this journey, how do you describe what you're written? What are these flaws?

Flaws are those activities that encourage the excess purchasing and consumption of material things. They support your bad habits by feeding into the attitudes and personality characteristics that promote the creation of debt.

This is what we are doing with pen and paper: isolating these flaws, detailing them, listing them in the FLAW Section of your 10-step book for critical success. Look over what you've written. Are you spending almost five hundred dollars a week on entertainment? Do you make eight hundred dollars a week? Is it reasonable for you to spend five hundred dollars a week on entertainment when you make eight hundred a week? If you've made it this far, I'm assuming you can answer this question using the smallest portion of your critical thinking skills.

Is your $600,000 house a flaw? Is your $55,000 car a flaw? Is your pinky ring a flaw? Are your shiny new rims a flaw? Is you cell phone bill a flaw? Is your cable bill a flaw? Do you even watch all those channels? Is your pizza and cheeseburger bill a flaw? Are you really buying fast food for lunch every day? Not only is it expensive, but it's also destructive to your body. IT'S A FLAW. These are all flaws.

Remember, question everything. Think critically about what you're doing. Look closely at each and every aspect of your life and determine what needs fixing through rigorous analysis and introspection. Know who you are and who you want to be and, more importantly, what you would like to achieve. Once you've completed this step, you'll be in full acceptance of your situation and prepared to make changes. You have a strong desire to be successful, and you know that in order to be successful you must fix what's broken in your life. You're ready for the next step. You're ready to fully utilize the tools.

CHAPTER 12
STEP 5: USE THE
TOOLS—3FE

And now we have arrived at the crux of the matter. In an effort to work my way through some critical challenges in the workplace, and at home—in order to find my way to financial security—I created a tool. I was well on my way to financial freedom before coming upon the tool. However, when I did discover it, I immediately began to put it to good use. Its creation was both enlightening and uplifting. It was incredibly simple and adhered to the tenets of critical thinking.

I refined this tool while working for who was perhaps the most demanding manager ever to grace the halls of my employer's office building. This woman was perhaps the most emphatic micro-manager in its history. *That's an emotional claim.* Let's dismiss the circumstances of how the tool was refined and get to it. We'll save that story for another day.

Critical Success: The 2 rules of 3 is the name of the program. We've worked our way halfway through the ten steps that lie at the heart of the program. The first four steps were all about self-analysis:

understanding who you are, what you have done, and why. Now we walk through a whole new door to a new vista and prepare to make changes.

This program of critical success speaks of the 2 rules of 3. The first rule is utilized in step five. The rule demands that you use the tool. The tool is 3FE. Now, what is 3FE? What is this tool that you will use to put together a plan that will be effective, satisfying, and gratifying?

3FE is the tool of *motivational empowerment*. Understand clearly that this means the tool, by design, will make you want to achieve. The very act of using the tool, of putting your plan together, is motivating. You immediately begin to feel a sense of achievement. After you walked through four steps that unearthed what was hidden and splayed open the financial wounds of your life, a tool is now thrust in your hand that is easy to use and will immediately make you feel empowered. Simply put, it will make you feel good! By using 3FE you are becoming a more powerful individual. You are a critical thinker marching clearly and confidently toward your own personal success. This is the power of 3FE.

3FE

FIND: Gather data. Seek. Leave no stone unturned.

FOCUS: Look at the gathered data with a discerning eye. Question the data. Construct relationships. Turn the data into meaningful information.

FUNDAMENTALS: Establish the **FUNDAMENTALS**. Examine the information thoroughly, changing what is applicable to the situation into actionable steps. **BUILD A PLAN!**

EXECUTE: Pull the trigger.

This tool is based in simplicity and designed for simple thinking. Applying it is motivating, and seeing its results is empowering. When I think of the utilization of the tool, I get excited. When I put the tool to use, I feel a strong sense of satisfaction and achievement. Just imagining you putting the tool to use excites me. Several phrases come to mind that speak to my excitement, *Fire for affect! Run and gun it! Work your project! Execute, execute, execute!* Yes, once you have utilized the tool, you will have a plan to follow. Execute it. Use it to build a plan for wealth and prosperity.

In the previous steps, we discussed the barriers to critical success, what they are, and why they are so important. Remember the barriers?

Lack of critical thinking skills
Media-driven Consumercelebreality
Willful assumption of debt
The get-rich-quick schemes

3FE is simple in explanation and implementation. However, if applied properly, it can be utilized to resolve the most complicated and convoluted problems. As we have already stated, 3FE is the tool of motivational empowerment. What do we mean when was say motivational? *Motivational* means something is motivating, and *motivating* means to incite, propel, provoke, prompt, or cause. What is empowerment? It means to give power or authority, invest with power, equip or supply with an ability, enable. When you utilize the tool, you follow a methodology. What is a methodology? It is a set of systems, or principles, and rules for regulating a given discipline, *such as the discipline of critical thinking*; an organized set of procedures or guidelines.

Let us combine what we have defined.

When utilizing 3FE, what we are doing is following established guidelines, which generate the potential for success by provoking individuals to action, creating a sense of empowerment. Maybe you think this is a bit farfetched. All I ask is that you stick to the steps, follow through on step five. Utilize the tool. Then judge for yourself.

Let's take a mental walk through the utilization of 3FE.

3FE stands for Find, Focus, establish the Fundamentals, and Execute. The tool is all about problem-solving. So you're faced with a problem, an issue, or what many like to call an opportunity. When you're in the thick of such an opportunity, you may be confused. You may be frustrated, exasperated. You may not be able to get your bearings or understand what's going around you. You're feeling overwhelmed. What is the first thing you must do? Can you guess? The very first thing you must do is the first step in the 10-point plan.

That's right, STOP and THINK!

Understand, not only must you stop and think. You must stop and think critically. You must take a deep breath, observe your surroundings, consider the situation, and start thinking about what's happening to you. Get the mental motor running. Start asking questions.

The tool is designed to be useful at varying levels of complexity. By breaking issues up into smaller units, you can apply the tool's central principles to problem-solving in units. By solving several smaller problems, you work your way to solving bigger ones. So you have a problem. No matter the complexity, you need it resolved. For our purposes, we're talking about the information you've gathered in steps three and four of the 10-point plan.

You're in the *find* phase of 3FE. You'll note that by working your way through steps one through four, you will have done a great deal of finding. You've listed, identified, and isolated. By working your way through the plan, you've pretty much accomplished the *find* phase. We know what we want to do. We want to establish F-PEC, fundamental personal economic control, in our lives. Have you correctly identified the problem? This too is part of the *find* phase. Overall we know the problem is debt, or no financial control, no budget, no plan. And, without a plan, we do indeed plan to fail.

In the *find* phase, we are all about gathering information; the more information, the better. However, you do have to be wary of information inundation. You can't get caught in phase paralysis, spending all your time finding more and more information but never addressing any of it. Gather your information and organize it. You can stop when you're sure you have a good grasp of the details at the high level. Don't delve deeply during this phase. Going through the plan enables you to do this effectively. As we've said, you've isolated what needs to be addressed; now it's time to move to the second phase of 3FE.

The *focus* phase is you conducting your in-depth analysis of the problem. You've defined the problem, issue, or opportunity. You're certain you know exactly what it is. Now it's time to start gathering all the facts. In order to work through this phase, I like to employ an analysis method I learned in the second grade. It's simple, practical, and eminently useful. It seems, as we get older, many of us forget to think about problem-solving in this manner. We forget the basics. When I *focus*, I try to remember to utilize 5WH. That is, I use the Five What's and How.

1. What
2. Who
3. When
4. Where
5. Why
6. How

Utilization of this analysis method lends itself naturally to 3FE. At any level of complexity, you can ask these six questions and discern facts, which will aid you in your resolution. Apply this in the focusing phase to the problem of your debt situation. You're talking about *what* bill, defining, redefining, and clarifying. You're talking about *who* made the bills. You're talking about *when* they were made and how frequently they arrive. You're talking about *where* the bills were made and *where* your funds are going, and you can even take the *where* further and talk about *who* is sucking up your money on this bill, *why*, and *how*—and *how* you may be able to alter the arrangement to better benefit your situation, like negotiating a lowering of interest rates, a consolidation, or payment program. You're talking about *why* you're paying these bills. You're working your way up into your mental calculus and asking critical questions. *Why am I paying this bill or any of these bills?* Are you trying to preserve your credit? Is the situation really dire? Is it time to move to the next level to seek assistance? Do you need to declare bankruptcy? Lastly, *how* is the bill affecting you and your family? *How is this bill being addressed?* Is it being addressed at all? Is the question, *how* do I address this god-awful, ass-biting, nut-crunching, pain-in-the-neck bill?

Focus, people. You must focus. Look at the picture you've painted of yourself and your situation. Look at what you've isolated. You have all the details before you. Focus on them and start discerning facts.

You'll find that moving through this exercise can be liberating. You will feel yourself moving forward, making changes. You will find that as you discern facts you'll start divining solutions. You almost can't help it. Your mind will move toward: *this is how I can fix this.* Or, at the very least, you'll start to acknowledge that you need to seek assistance in resolving the situation. This takes us into the third phase of 3FE.

Establishing the *fundamentals* is the downward slope of 3FE. Once you've completed the *find* and *focus* phases, you'll realize that you may be moving more rapidly toward resolution, almost like a downhill slope. If you're not moving downhill, you'll feel you've reached a plateau and you're leveling out. I don't want to diminish the importance of this phase. It is just as important as the first two. However, I want to emphasize that if you have moved through the first two, you're really going with gas. You can readily make the jump to the next phase.

Establishing the *fundamentals* is about putting together your plan. It's about making connections between the facts you've discerned in the *focus* phase. It's about building structure around the information you gathered in the *find* phase. How does this apply to our objective of establishing F-PEC?

In order to establish the *fundamentals*, you must take the facts and details and consider their relationship to the problem or problems you've defined. You must also consider the relationships between the facts themselves. Peel the onion in this phase. If you have to do more focusing on a given fact, then do so. However, be wary of analysis paralysis. This is where you continue to analyze a problem over and over and never move toward a resolution. As it pertains to our financial situation, establishing the *fundamentals* is about seeing how paying one bill affects another bill or how saving a certain amount of money monthly affects your overall financial picture.

For F-PEC, we quickly move to a solution-oriented mode of thinking. Realize that the *fundamentals* you need to detail in this phase are how to pay. How do you correct? How do you solve the problem? You have all the details before you. You have a wealth of information to work with. What must you do? You must put together a plan. The *fundamentals* are the actions you will take to resolve the problem, fix the issue, and take advantage of the opportunity.

Write down how you will resolve the problem. If you come up with multiple ways to resolve your financial problems, write them all down. We're picking and choosing here. Some of the things you may write down may simply be statements about the situation. *Paying off the furniture bill will require an additional $150 dollars a month for six months. Where will the money come from? You know what? I really don't need cable.*

Look over all the fundamental statements you have made. Understand clearly how your *fundamentals* relate to the problem. Understand clearly how they may be able to resolve the problem. Now, if you have not already done so, use your VERBS. Make sure what you're written is actionable. Organize them into steps.

1) I will research how to structure a budget.
2) I will create a budget.
3) I will open a savings account.
4) I will commit $100 a month to it.
5) I will open an IRA (investment retirement account).
6) I will commit $200 a month to it.

You have numbered your statements. They are actionable. They say you are going to actually DO something. These steps will become your fundamental plan. Your fundamental plan was the goal of this entire phase. Now focus on your plan. Refine it. Make changes where you feel they are necessary. You must own this plan from beginning to end. You must make it work for you. It must be the type of plan that lets you see yourself living with a large degree of financial security in a specified amount of time. Will it take you one year, two years, or five years to get out of debt? Your plan should reflect this timetable. It should have milestone dates for achieving smaller tactical objectives as part of your larger strategic goal.

1) Put an extra $200 into Visa bill.
2) Change cell phone plans for lower monthly rate.
3) Cut off cable.
4) Turn in overpriced, pain-in-the-ass luxury car that we leased.
5) Buy a used car to get from A to B.

6) Start conducting research to see if it would be better to sell the house and move into something more affordable.
7) Milestone date 12/15: pay off Visa bill. (MERRY CHRISTMAS!)
8) Assess F-PEC status on 1/5, after holiday hoopla.

For those of you familiar with Microsoft Project, your plan can become quite detailed if you feel it is necessary. Some of you may truly require this type of attention to detail. Microsoft Project allows you to create a project schedule. This schedule tracks your activities. It numbers and details tasks; allows you to list how long a task will take, on what day it will start, and on what day it will finish; assigns someone to a task; and marks those oh-so-important milestone dates. For those of you without Project or the skills to use it, you can create your own project schedule in a spreadsheet, or even on a piece of paper. You need nothing more than the tasks and dates and the knowledge of who's doing what and how long it will take to complete.

Once you have your plan, you are there! You are on your way! You are green go, and going with gas! Why do I say this? Why do I feel good when I say it? I feel good when I say it because you now have a plan that you can utilize to move closer to critical success. You are ready for the final phase of 3FE. It's so simple. It's so appropriate. To be in the last phase requires that you take that fateful step: utilize the momentum and enthusiasm you've built and EXECUTE.

I may be making it sound too easy. Please don't misunderstand me. Getting to this point required a tremendous amount of effort. Pulling the trigger on your plan is just the beginning. Now you have to stick to the plan. It may be hard. You may waver. However, when you do, remember you have a plan and your plan leads to a goal. You must remain diligent and true to what you've put together. This is your plan, divined through critical thinking. It's yours. You own it. You know if you follow it you will achieve success. Do not waver. If you do waver, return to the plan. Always return to the plan.

Now, I want you to know that establishing the *fundamentals* can be the most difficult thing you ever do. I may have made it sound too easy. For some this will be true. By just arriving at step five, they may already have some idea of the drastic measures they may have to take to establish F-PEC. Others may come to step five feeling good about their achievements thus far but with no idea about the *fundamentals*. They may be flying blind, unable to see a direction. And finally, there will be those who see a direction. It's murky, foggy, and scary, and they will not want to move forward. I would like to help all of you overcome this barrier to critical success. Do you know what it requires?

It requires critical thinking, of course.

Allow me to vent. In my venting, I'm going to offer you all what many consider drastic options to achieving F-PEC. However, if your situation is dire, you need to consider them. You've painted your picture. You know what you've done. You may understand you're a victim, infected by MDC. Critical thinking is your antibiotic. It will allow you to cure yourself, if you have the stomach for the medicine. Know this: for many of you, if you want to truly achieve critical success, you will have to throw off MDC, think critically, and do the hard things. What are the hard things?

Okay, venting …

The National Foundation for Credit Counseling, also known as Consumer Credit Counseling Services, or CCCS, may be your first and only stop. It's entirely up to you. Personally I don't trust anyone else. There are many credit counseling and debt consolidation services out there, but this is the only one I believe in. It's a nonprofit that is dedicated to helping you eradicate your debt. Please, go to the website, www.nfcc.org, and locate a CCCS member agency near you.

For those of you who are like I was—stupid and spoonish, sopping up MDC, spending money, and imbibing on clothes, restaurants, drink, and good times—this is strong medicine. I went to them and with their help put together a budget that would have me debt free in five years.

People, we need to change the way we think. There is no stigma in thinking critically and doing what you must to achieve F-PEC. If you have to cut up all your cards, and go to CCCS, then do so, and do it today. If you have to sell your stupidly overpriced house, which you bought with an interest-only loan, then do so, and do it today. TAKE THE DAMN LEX COUPE, BEEMER, OR BENZ back to the goddamn dealership, and do it today!

BANKRUPTCY IS NOW AN OPTION!

I say again, bankruptcy is now an option! For those of you who hate the thought of such a stigma, let it go! Stop and think! Start thinking critically! Will you have to declare bankruptcy? I hope not, but if through your research, rationalization, and critical thinking, you've logically determined this is your best option, DON'T HESITATE! ACT! This is war, people! That's right. It's us against MDC and the nefarious forces that push the disease on us at the expense of all our futures, including their own, in their ignorant shortsightedness.

I am a strong advocate of entrepreneurship, capitalism, and the struggle for individual success. However, I am also a strong advocate of unity, teams, and the distribution of blessings, as we are able to or as they may be earned, but not at the expense of personal motivation and self-improvement.

With that understanding, I still say I am extremely disappointed in the people who lead our world and sustain our popular culture. MDC is the disease. Critical thinking is the cure. However, there are those in power who will do what they can to pass laws and institute policies that limit your ability to achieve critical success, if you remain spoonish and a victim of MDC.

They think it's okay to charge you 28 percent interest. They revel in their success at passing laws to limit your ability to file for bankruptcy. Granted, you may have been a stone-cold idiot for getting into such a mess, but what good will it do any of us if you remain a victim of MDC, mired in debt. You'll simply be a burden on society, one of the many rapidly working their way toward making their home on a park bench.

Listen, seven years is not a bad price to pay for low blood-pressure, freedom from stress, and a plan for the future. If through your 3FE exercise you find that you must file for bankruptcy, then you must do so, and you must do it today. If you can't liquidate, then try debt restructuring. If you can't do that, screw it; stop paying on the credit cards. Concentrate on keeping a roof over your head and food in your family's mouth. Tell the card companies to go to HELL.

Know this—and it is the truth: if you file bankruptcy, the moment your bankruptcy is discharged, the mongers will come a-calling. You will receive offers in the mail for loans and credit cards. Yes, they will come back. They'll suggest you do a prepaid card. They'll tell you it will be of great benefit. They want to give you money and catch you in the same trap all over again. I've said it before and I'll say it again: PEOPLE, LIFE DOES NOT TAKE VISA—OR MASTERCARD, OR DISCOVER, OR AMERICAN EXPRESS! You got cash and a checkbook? Then you're good!

Visa is a tool that enables you to choose. You have options with VISA. However, if you use VISA for something, make sure you're prepared to pay it back as soon as possible. Now understand, the credit card companies don't like it when you pay them back on time. The love it when you make those little payments, just barely covering the interest. They love to string you out over a number of years. You're guaranteed income. Don't be guaranteed income for someone else. Put your money to work for you. I have plenty of credit cards. I like my credit cards. No, I actually love them. However, I use them responsibly. I want the system to work. I want the credit card companies to make money off of me, but only what they should be entitled to for the service they are providing, nothing more.

Use the tool. Examine your life thoroughly. Think critically about who you are, what you're doing, who you want to be, and what you want to accomplish. Apply 3FE to your life today. Remember to document all your work in your ten-step book for critical success. Build a plan that will lead you to critical success!

*Note: Be wary of the OLH factor. The *oh life happens* factor affects us all. Just when you think you've made it, and you're a month away from paying off your last bill, you get a new one for increased property taxes, or your car's transmission goes down. Oh, yes, life happens. As a rule of thumb, take any estimate you make about how long it will take you to get out of debt and double it. At the very least, add a few months. This will set your expectations at an appropriate level and will quite possibly allow you to reach your goal much earlier than expected based on this new expectation. It will make you feel good.

CHAPTER 13
STEP 6: UNDERSTAND THE 3 PRINCIPLES OF PROSPERITY (3PoP)

The second rule in the 2 rules of 3 is as simple as the first, or rather as simple as it needs to be in order for you to apply it. It's all about you taking full advantage of the opportunities that will become open to you once you fully embrace the critical success way of life. If you pursue your critical success and maintain your level of discipline with the passion of a world-class athlete, then you will come to a time and place in your personal journey when the second rule must apply. It will be a great moment. You will go back to the first step in the 10-Point plan and realize with no small amount of joy that the world is yours—that success is right there, waiting for you. You can take it.

So ... what is the second rule?

Rule 2: Understand the 3 Principles of Prosperity (3PoP)

1) Invest in real estate.
2) Invest in the financial markets.
3) Become an entrepreneur.

Every person working toward achieving critical success must understand that 3PoP must play a critical role in achieving that success. Knowing, acknowledging, and attempting to implement what the rule implies means that you will cover the gamut of financial opportunities our modern culture has to offer.

The rule requires that you invest in real estate. The rule requires that you invest in the market. The rule requires that you become an entrepreneur. The first principle requires you to acquire some land. Work on the land that is available. I don't necessarily mean grow your own corn. However, if you do literally work the land, then use the 3FE tool to discover more innovative ways to get your produce to market. However, as for the rest of us non-farmers, work on owning land. Every person should strive to own more then one piece of land.

Now, I demand that you respect the land—that you do acknowledge that although you may own the land legally, bequeath it to others, pass it on to children, or sell it for a profit, the land belongs to the Earth, and the Earth belongs to posterity. We're tenants, each generation in our own turn. Treat the land you do come to own through legal documentation as though it is one of your most precious possessions, because it is.

On another note, choose a parcel of land to live on. This will be your home. You will live here. You will love here. You will raise children here. The house you erect on the land you choose to call home is one of your most sacred possessions. You must protect it for your family and for those with whom you choose to share it. Don't be stupid and try to turn your home into an investment. It can drive you crazy. Don't run yourself ragged trying to force an increase in its value and use it as a bank. Your home is not a credit card, no matter how hard the financial mongrels try to convince you otherwise. YOUR LIFE DOES NOT TAKE VISA! Sorry, it just came out. Listen, your home is not an investment. It is where you live. There is a difference.

Invest some of your money in the financial markets. The second principle requires you to be an investor in stocks and bonds. Don't be spoonish and become a stock market junkie. Don't gamble away your hard-earned cash. Wall Street can be even more cutthroat than Vegas. As with anything you undertake, you must apply critical thinking skills. In order to invest in the markets, you must become educated, and not a little bit savvy. Here's the thing: don't you think it wise to have an understanding of what you're doing with your money? Would you give your money to a crackhead? Of course not—at least I hope not. Don't just turn over your cash to some mutual fund manager who doesn't give a damn about how important your $40,000 nest egg is to you and your family. Be discerning. Be critical thinking.

You must invest in the market.

However, you shall not invest without the requisite education. I state that as a demand. It is a demand you must place on yourself. When it comes to investing your money, you will be informed. You will ask questions. If you open an account with a broker that allows you to trade stocks, then take the time to learn about it. Read books. Talk to other people who do their own investing. If you do choose to let someone manage your investments, study them just like you would read the book. Look at their past performance. Learn all you can about the company. And still read the book. If you do decide to do a little day trading, limit the amount of money you're willing to put into play. DO NOT LEVERAGE YOUR RETIREMENT MONEY ON A HOT STOCK TIP. This is the most spoonish of behaviors. I know. I've done it. Pure stupidity. Believe me.

The third principle is the best of them all. If you follow principles one and two and you're diligent and stick to the plan, I guarantee you, major disasters not withstanding, you will be secure in your retirement. You will be financially sound as a pound (hmm, depending on the current exchange rate, and whether the pound is still around) well before your retirement. However, if you truly want to try to circumvent the long way toward financial security—if you think you have a good idea, if you think you're an innovator, if you like to take risks—then just maybe the way of the entrepreneur is for you. The third principle is the true heart of wealth creation. Becoming an entrepreneur is the tried and true way of making tens of millions of dollars in wealth.

Go ahead. Give it a shot. If your heart and mind are up to it, try starting a business. Now, you have to be careful. When I say take risks, I don't mean risk everything. Do not—I repeat, do not—take all the wealth you worked so hard to build using principles one and two and bet it all on a kid's Bounce, Play 'n' Stay Franchise. Don't bet it all on any franchise. Don't spend all your hard-earned money on some crazy invention that you think will make you billions of dollars. I have experience in this area. Trust me, it's always best to stop, think, plan, and then execute. Don't throw your money into a mom-and-pop chicken shop next to a Chik-Fil-A. You'll get creamed! Entrepreneurship may be for you, but certainly only critical thinkers need apply. If you believe this is truly your passion, then the third principle is definitely for you. Critical success prepares you for the challenge of discovering your inner entrepreneur. Do you have a great idea? Do you have a new process? Have you discovered an unexploited niche in an established market? Remember to use the first rule as you apply the third principle. 3FE your way to success. Realize your dream. Pursue the third principle with true passion and become the world's next great success story!

For you budding entrepreneurs, I recommend reading *The E-Myth Revisited* by Michael Gerber. It gave my friends and I a new perspective on concepts we already knew and understood. We also gained a wealth of knowledge by clarifying how we should approach starting a business. It's an easy-to-understand read, very compelling in its implications, and 100 percent actionable. You will come away from this book with very real action items and to-dos.

And of course, don't forget the most important part. Take your thoughts on 3PoP and add them to the next section of your 10-step book for critical success. You can use this section and come back to it time and time again to look over how your thoughts on prosperity change as you journey down the path toward critical success.

CHAPTER 14
STEP 7: KNOW THE
CLEAR DISCIPLINE OF
EFFECTIVE EXECUTION

You're not beginning to do a good job until you've asked yourself, what can I do better today? As you should recall from chapter two, this sentence is one of my many mantras. I keep it hanging on my wall, and I say it every day at work. It helps to keep me focused. If I've completed a job, a may take a deep breath and pause. However, you can be sure I'm going to glance over at my mantra and consider what's next on my to-do list. Is this really a good stopping point? Should I commit that extra bit of effort to make the day successful above and beyond the norm? Should I?

At the very least, I consider it. I would recommend you do the same. This may be difficult, but completion of your tasks, be they self-assigned or assigned by someone else, is a great reward. You feel good when you've finished completing your assigned tasks. You feel good when you're working on a plan, *especially your plan for critical success*, and you've reached a milestone. The feeling is tremendous. With this feeling of tremendous success being your reward, you must *know the clear discipline of effective execution.*

What does this mean?

As you move from step seven to step eight, you must acknowledge that all the work you've been doing for steps one through seven created a shift in the way you think. As you've completed each step, you've remained focused. You've established the fundamentals. This required an altered state of mind. By remaining committed to the goal of completing the ten steps, you've remained disciplined. You've followed a path that has been outlined for you to flesh out and complete. Executing those steps effectively requires discipline and commitment. As you move from step to step, you feel a sense of accomplishment; you feel good.

As you do for the ten steps, so must you do for your life.

Let's contemplate the word *discipline* for a moment. It has a strong connotative meaning. It sounds hard. It feels difficult. Sometimes we equate it with pain. We may say it with our lips thinned, our teeth gnashed together, and a hiss of air. You may remember the terse word, the switch, and for some of you few and proud, even the barking drill sergeant. However, you will remember that when you experienced these modes of discipline, there was a goal in mind, an objective. In order to achieve it, you had to be disciplined.

It doesn't have to be painful. But sometimes it is. You may endure actual physical pain, like backache as you finish the drywall in your investment property. However, you will persevere. You have a goal. You will finish the task that leads to property. You may struggle. You leveraged a good deal of money on this investment, these cars you have for resale, and you see the payout; it's just coming far too slowly. It's taking too long for you to fix up the Mustangs. You have to cut back on your expenses. You have to live a little lean. You may even have to get a second job. However, you have a plan. Your returns on the cars are going to get you that little apartment building you have been eyeing. You have to stay the course, remain disciplined. Follow the plan and do not stray from your goal.

Know the clear discipline of effective execution.

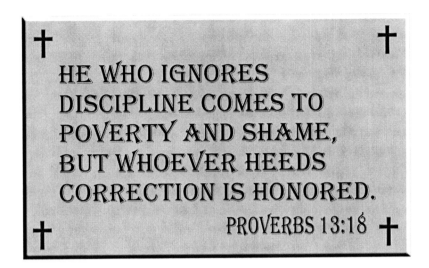

HE WHO IGNORES DISCIPLINE COMES TO POVERTY AND SHAME, BUT WHOEVER HEEDS CORRECTION IS HONORED.
PROVERBS 13:18

Few of us in the world are truly lucky. The rest of us think, plan, and work very hard in order to succeed. You must have the discipline to see it through. It is a contest of wills; you against the odds, you against likely failure, you against the world. You must be determined not to fail. Oprah Winfrey is fond of saying that she doesn't believe in luck—that success is in truth what happens when proper preparation meets opportunity. I happen to agree with her.

As I stated in the introductory booklet, today far too many people no longer believe in discipline. They approach life with the wrong attitude. They don't practice patience. They are acolytes of *immediate gratification.* They want everything now, and they expect it to be given to them in some form or fashion that is conducive to their lackadaisical, over-weighted, fat-brained and bodied, deep-dish, spoon-like lifestyles. This is the legacy of the debt-burdened modern pop culture. Indeed Prince did say it: "pop life, what's the matter with your world!"

If you are going to achieve critical success, you most know the clear discipline of effective execution. Through the utilization of the first rule, you have devised a plan for yourself that structures your life properly for the march toward achieving success. Through the power of 3FE, you will take advantage of available financial opportunities for the accumulation of personal wealth, establishing F-PEC along the way. You will facilitate growth by adhering to 3PoP, the three principles of prosperity. Next week you're closing on the purchase of your quadplex, plus one duplex, and a single-family home for rehab and resale. You have a plan and will execute it effectively, with specific intent. You will succeed!

However, in order to achieve success, you must be disciplined. You must remain clear in mind as it pertains to the execution of tasks. You must remain focused on the task. When your mind gets cluttered, you must stop and think critically. Question what's going on. Why are you losing focus? Why is your mind cluttered? Quickly analyze the situation and rectify it. Get back on course. Move forward with your plan. Stick to your steps—these steps that are clearly defined and will lead you to success. You know this because you've gone over your plan hundreds of times, just to make sure you've got it right. Executing your effective plan aids you in remaining disciplined. You will not deviate from your good, strong plan without good, strong, valid reasons. And these reasons must be established through rigorous questioning and the application of critical thinking. Throughout your journey, you must remain patient. You must remain disciplined.

Before moving on to the next chapter, you need to complete your written account of activities during this step. You know the drill. Write down how you know the clear discipline of effective execution in your 10-step book for critical success. Tell a story. Write a list. What tasks are you doing on a daily basis to remain disciplined and committed? What obstacles have you overcome? How did you overcome them? What is the story of your disciplined and effective execution?

CHAPTER 15
STEP 8: WHY DO WE FALL? SO WE CAN GET BACK UP AGAIN!

Life is an unending struggle. Fate is a pretentious bastard. He makes demands and stands as the avatar of Destiny, who is nothing more than a crotchety old crone. They are two sides of the same coin, and they refuse to be read, dictated to, understood, predicted, affected, or changed. You can't predict the future, because the future is unknown. It's just that simple. However, you can plan.

You can believe in the future you've worked to create. You can execute flawlessly. You can be the captain of your destiny and the master of your fate. And just when you think all is right with the world and you are king "whoever you are," the ruler of all you survey, that bastard Fate and his crotchety mistress Destiny conspire with a disgustingly chaotic and contrarian universal variable called Murphy, to totally crap on all your beautiful plans and flawless execution.

As they say, *the best laid plans of mice and men.*

You must learn to acknowledge failure. You must understand the rule of failure. Smashing headlong into failure makes us despondent; makes us angry, sad, listless, even doomed. It makes us want to quit. It's at these times that we must remember step seven and know the clear discipline of effective execution. Revamp your plan. Conduct a 3FE analysis on why you failed. Adopt an attitude that says, "I will never quit, as long as I can find a way." Use whatever tools are at your disposal to make sure that as you fall, you're ready to get right back up again. Read "Attitude," pray, or use the Secret.

A point of order for those of you out there who believe in the power of the Secret: I've covered some of this ground already, but I would like to add a bit more. The authors of *The Secret* state that you can have whatever you want, no matter what. They say that the universe will bend to your will. I'm not a scientist, theologian, or mystic. I'm just a common man with common sense. From this common standpoint, I would say there is truly something to human rationality, our power of cognition, as well as the power of human emotions, love, faith, and prayer. *The Secret* teaches us about the law of attraction. It teaches us to view the universe as Aladdin's genie in the lamp. This is very important to consider where the rule of failure is concerned. Suppose I'm crafting the universe according to my design and I'm bending reality using all my will, all my power of belief. Suppose you're using the Secret, you're my neighbor, and you're crafting the universe to your design, bending reality using all your will and all your power of belief. What do you suppose happens when our realities are diametrically opposed and they come into conflict? We can't both have the universe bend to our will in the same space, can we? I'll answer for you. No, we cannot. What we get is chaos. How does this chaos manifest itself? It manifests itself as failure. Just a thought for you Secret folks out there.

And so, back to our main point. Let's say you're a disciplined planner who knows how to remain committed. You're a critical thinker who takes the time to examine a given situation. You question everything. You listen and you learn. You see your way to success. You know what drives you. You know your passions. You know what will make you happy. You even have accepted the fact that achieving critical success will take approximately six years, five to get out of debt and the sixth to start your market investment portfolio and your real estate acquisition plan. You have it all mapped out to the letter.

Six months into your plan, it all comes apart. It crashes down around you. You're a thirty-seven-year-old man dreaming of success, critical success. Now all you have are ashes. You can't help it; the tears come. Sometimes even a grown man has to cry.

What do you do?

You fall and then you simply get back up. It's as simple as it sounds—for the most part. Unfortunately, as human beings churning with emotion, picking ourselves back up after a failure can be one of the most difficult things we will ever do. However, it can and must be done. How do we know that it must be done? The rule of failure tells us it must be done. And what does the rule of failure say? It simply states: YOU WILL FAIL!

You must understand the rule of failure. From the rule of failure you come to understand why we must define why we fall and why it is imperative to insist that we only fall in order to get back up again. With our own will, we make it an aphorism that must be lived by those who seek to achieve critical success.

If you think critically about failure, you will realize that even if you give your all to everything you try to do, you cannot always be successful. It just can't happen. Understand, the world is wonderful and varied, and there may very well exist those few lucky people who never fail. They're special. If you're one of them, you should start writing about yourself today. If you're not one of these very special, almost assuredly nonexistent people, then you're like the rest of us, and you must learn to cope with failure.

I have a favorite T-shirt that I like to wear that pretty much sums up my opinion on failure. It picked it up when I visited NASA's Johnson Space Center in Houston, Texas. I really love that place. The men and women of NASA have a saying, which is printed on the front of my T-shirt: *failure is not an option*. This motto is very important to me because it exemplifies the right attitude. It is what we must aspire to. Understand, we all know that NASA is very familiar with the concept of failure. However, they by no means accept it. They do not let it stop them dead in their tracks. No, if it occurs, they accept it, learn from it, and move past it.

Consider your local physician. You doctor also knows failure. However, just as it is for NASA, failure for doctors is not an option. They have to live their lives committed to the concept of not failing and thereby not doing harm, as the heart of their Hippocratic oath. Yet doctors do fail. It is an awesome and humbling responsibility. However, they must maintain the right attitude, accept what happens, and move on in order to try to save the next life, and the next life, and the next life. They must have the right attitude, no matter the emotional cost.

Dealing with failure is just as important as how you deal with success. Both require you to think critically. Both require you to temper your approach. Both require you to have a proper attitude. Most of us never learn how to deal with failure effectively. When we try to succeed—when we give it everything we have and then a little extra, when we sweat blood and tears, when we drive ourselves to exhaustion, putting all our heart, mind, and soul into our objective—and fail, we are totally devastated.

Being devastated is natural. If you weren't devastated after a spectacular failure, I would be inclined to think something was wrong with you. However, it is critical that you digest your failure, analyze it, and then begin to move past it.

After you have had a moment to feel sorry for yourself (remember, perfectly natural), you must pick yourself up. You must center your mind, your body, and, yes, even your soul. You must steel yourself for what comes next and begin again. Use the power of 3FE. If your objective is to get right back in the mix and succeed at the very same thing you just failed at, then *find* where you failed and why. *Focus* on it. Establish the *fundamentals* associated around this particular issue and build your plan of attack. Then, once you're ready, *execute*.

If you try to apply 3FE after a spectacular failure and you're still moping and sad or angry and mad, scattered in thought, and not directed, you will simply fail again. You have to approach this with the right attitude. You might even want to start with a smile. I know this sounds silly, but I can't begin to tell you how powerful a smile can be—a smile and the proper attitude.

I was an awful student. I had what was called potential. My mother saw it and fostered it. She involved me in summer camp

117

reading programs, extracurricular activities, scouts, everything to expand my horizons. Even though I had every advantage, I still failed. I didn't concentrate in class. I didn't apply myself. I've always had people who believed in me. However, I continued to disappoint. I continued to fail. Still, due to my attitude, I continued to inspire and present hope, and for me personally, I continued to dream.

In 1995 I was hired by a tech company as an entry-level analyst/ programmer. I got the job because I showed promise in my interview. Again I inspired with a positive attitude. The salary was $35,000, and for this I dropped out of the University of Georgia with three courses left to complete. During my first performance review, the man who hired me told me I was a terrible disappointment. I was a failure. He said I would not be receiving a salary increase, because I was an underperformer. I thought he was going to fire me. Instead he simply asked me to sign my name on my review and told me to go back to work.

In the meantime, I was dreaming. I tried to start a business on my own. It was a bust. I got into real estate. While I was doing this, I was planning my eventual conquest of the stock market by day trading. I failed at this miserably. How bad did I fail? I lost tens of thousands of dollars. I went into monstrous debt.

So, in my estimation, things were looking bad. I still lived with my parents, even though I owned rental homes. I had borrowed on credit to play in the stock market and was barely making the minimum monthly payments. I was always broke. I was drinking more and more. Basically I was a complete failure, a dropout with no prospects and too much debt to make it from month to month. I was feeling pretty low.

What did I do? Well, first I looked at the poem that I kept above my desk at home. I read "Attitude" by Charles Swindoll. It had always been my mainstay, helping me maintain a positive attitude and spurring me onward. However, I was a constantly smiling, upbeat, daydreaming, always-looking-for-a-shortcut, wanna-be-rich-in-less-than-a-week drunk. There was no way in hell I was headed for a successful *anything*! Now I was changing gears. I needed to apply my positive attitude to my efforts at critical thinking. I needed to fix my situation.

So, what did I do? Why, 3FE of course.

I didn't need to *find* the problem. It was staring me in the face. I needed to manage my debt. I *focused*, put together my plan from the *fundamentals*, and *executed*. I applied for consumer credit counseling so I could get my credit debt negotiated to reasonable payment levels. In the meantime, I put my rental property up for sale. I dumped all my get-rich schemes and decided to focus on my career at work. I had been doing much better since that first year, but I knew I really needed to push in order to be seen as a person who could be successful and lead. I wanted to get promoted. Finally I reapplied to the University of Georgia (UGA). It was time for me to finish school and get my degree. I had my plan and I lived it. My homes sold quickly. I made enough money to pay off all my debt from day trading. In 2000 I graduated from UGA eleven years after I started. It took a long time, but I can't tell you how good it felt. Before my father died, I was able show him an official UGA diploma with his son's name on it. I made him very proud. Seeing the smile on his face was one of the greatest moments of my entire life.

I failed, but I did not wallow in my failure for long. I turned it around. I became a success. What does the rule of failure state? The rule of failure states that *you will fail*. However, you can use the tools at your disposal to turn failure into success. Failure does not have to be a permanent condition. The example of my life is small and one of many. Look around you. There are plenty of examples of people turning failure into success every day. No matter the challenge, no matter the obstacle, meet it squarely, face to face. Lift your chin, set your shoulders, plant your feet, brace yourself. You may fail, but you may conquer. See it through.

Document your failures. Take the time to gather your thoughts and write down how you dealt with them. You know the drill. This is all part of your 10-step book for critical success. List your plans for addressing your failures and getting back on track. This section is very important because it recounts how you pushed aside feelings of failure and worthlessness and forged on to see it through. Whether it's a paragraph, an essay, or pictures and images, gather it all together and put it in your book as part of your critical success story.

CHAPTER 16
STEP 9: FOLLOW THE
YELLOW BRICK ROAD

A state of mind.

As I've said, your state of mind is critically important. You must consider it. Is it all about champagne wishes and caviar dreams? Can you follow the yellow brick road to your very own Emerald City, resplendent with the latest accoutrements? Crap, people! That's all a bunch of crap. Shifting your mind to dreaming of the cars, clothes, and caviar may suit some people. They may believe that the best way to reach your objective is to constantly dream about the day when you can purchase your very own Bentley. You know what I say? Bull! This is nothing more than a symptom of MDC, media-driven consumercelebreality tactically pushed into your face to convince you to purchase whatever crap on a dish they're shoveling your way. Don't fall for it.

Again, it's a state of mind—in particular a proper state of mind.

As you've worked your way through the ten steps, you may come to realize that your happiness, your success, and your wealth may very well include a glass of champagne and caviar, if you like fish eggs. I know I do. However, they do not define my success. I don't see these purchases as my objective. My yellow brick road does not lead to an Emerald City. Instead it leads to an open horizon, uncluttered by financial encumbrances and emotional obstacles of the past.

The yellow brick road is very real, and it exists on the other side of a door in your mind. If you're doing the right things, if you're thinking critically and working toward your objectives, you will have opened that door in your mind, walked through, and will be on your way down the road before you even realize you've started. The road may be long and winding, but you can get to the end. It will be different for each of us, giving us joy and pain to suit our characters and experiences. However, we can all reach the end.

The truth of the yellow brick road is that if you believe in it, if you're thinking critically about what you want—what your spirit really needs to achieve happiness—then just as the Great Wizard of Oz led the Cowardly Lion to the truth of his own courage, you will know and understand your own truth: that you're already walking the road of gold, well on your way to critical success.

You will move swiftly through the tasks that you have assigned yourself and others. Your plan, established as part of your 3FE analysis, may have started with some difficulty, but as you think critically about each task, and move closer and closer to your first, second, or maybe even your final milestone, you will begin to notice that things are running like a well-oiled machine. You're thinking clearly. You're achieving goals. You're completing tasks. Yes, you're on the road of gold. In your mind, you see your objective, and you're as certain you're going to achieve it as surely as Friday comes at the end of every workweek.

You are a critical thinker with a plan. You know what drives you. You know what you need. You are walking the path. In your mind, when you look down, you smile. Beneath your feet, which are steadily moving forward toward your goal, a soft glow rises from the road. There are smooth spots and cracks. Sometimes the road breaks. You find the detour. However, the beautiful thing about the road is that whenever you look down, you smile. The glow rises, and it's gold.

Now what is your state of mind? Write down how you feel. Imagine your yellow brick road and detail what comes to mind. Express your freedom to metaphorically walk the road in words.

America once had a reputation around the world for being paved with streets of gold. It wasn't a literal truth. It was a metaphor for opportunity. Today, as it was then, America is the best country in the world for opportunity. If you're not in America, think critically about where you are and what you're doing. I can't stress this enough. Think critically about what's available to you; think about your opportunities. Through the forests, jungle, thickets, and brambles, can you see the edge of the wood? And in your mind's eye, can you perceive the beginning of the road?

It is an attitude. It is a state of mind.

CHAPTER 17
STEP 10: WALK
INTO THE CLEAR

And so we come to the final step. It is through this last step that you will reach critical success. However, please do understand that one pass of this information is not enough. The creation of your 10-step book for critical success is not enough. You must take the time to review the material. Your book must become worn, dog-eared at the edges, as you refer to it again and again. Come back to the pages in this book frequently to refresh your mind and draw inspiration. You will achieve success. Use this book, and the book of your own design, to continuously fuel your mind. Use it to uplift your spirit and bolster your will. For those of you with an abiding belief in a higher power, take these words and relate them to your *good book*. Pray, those of you who believe in the power of prayer. Wish and call upon the universe, those of you who use the Secret. For you agnostics or atheists, stay strong, remain motivated, and above all, be passionate.

In these last pages of your 10-step book, write down how good it feels to be free. That's what step ten is all about. You're free—free to be silly, if you so desire. Unfortunately, right now, most of us can't afford to be silly. The cost is just too high. However, by working to be in step ten, we seek to be free enough to enjoy life and be silly whenever we so desire. We become the example for others.

Whether it has taken one year or ten years, you are now free. You have followed your plan, walked along your gilded road, and reached the end. Before you is the open vista, the clear horizon. You take a step forward and then another into the great green-and-blue. The sun is shining. It's beautiful, and you are free.

What will you do?

That is the power of arriving at step ten and moving forward. What will you do with the money you've been putting aside just for this purpose? You have established F-PEC, fundamental personal economic control. You are not a whale of debt. Your debt has been completely eliminated. Your bills are paid. You sleep with a smile on your face because you've been walking the golden road for some years. You've taken action with 3PoP, building a financial future while eliminating debt.

You own your own home, and you've purchased a duplex as rental property. You've opened an IRA. You've started an investment portfolio. You became so intrigued with the stock market that you opened an online trading account and started buying stocks on your own.

However, you're very critical of what you buy and sell. You are no day trader and have no desire to become one. You're not looking for the quick win. You're learning the equity markets, and you're having a good time doing it.

Your two children are well taken care of. You've established 529 plans for their college education. You've taken to discussing the importance of critical thinking with them. You have them reading *An Educational Primer for the Majority Student*. You tell them they're going to be Capital Graduates.

You stop and think, and you realize ... you have achieved critical success.

Now you have the room to truly consider 3PoP. You've been thinking about the three principles and you really want to see what you can do. You want to stretch and reach for an even higher level of critical success. You're free. You can do whatever you like. Do you start something new? You can. And that's what's beautiful. It's time to choose a course of action, firm up the fundamentals, and execute.

As you embark upon your new journey, truly exploring the many options of 3PoP, you must learn to TAKE THE LONG VIEW. As you grow as a critical thinker, you will find that this has already become natural to you. When you consider investment for your retirement and fund savings plans for you children's education, you're taking the long view.

You are a steward. Whether you are royalty, a merchant, or a happy peasant, you are a steward. We are not in this world forever, and it is our responsibility to try to leave it better than we found it. That means planning to take care of yourself and not becoming a burden to the world. That means being the best you, with the ability to render aide, guide others.

As part of *walking into the clear*, you look to the future. You look beyond yourself. You consider your family and your community, the extension of you. You consider your descendants. What will you leave behind? What will be your contribution to the world our children inherit? How will you benefit the community? During this journey, have you learned to think critically, to improve yourself? Now it is time to share what you have become and work to improve the world around you.

You will come to realize that becoming the best you involves intimate interaction with others. You will not know true joy until you realize the benefit of selfless giving. And when it comes to selfless giving, you have no worries, because you can truly afford to give. You would have given nonetheless, but it's nice to know that giving won't hurt so much in the pocket.

And your reward?

When you see your good works, financial or otherwise, benefit someone in need, something inside your soul stirs and begins to shine. Personally I believe this is a gift from God. It is the realization of that which is best within ourselves. However, you cannot begin to approach this horizon of clear thinking and action until you adequately equip yourself to do so. You must be the best you and offer the best of you to someone else. That's what the ten steps of the

10-point plan are all about: helping you discover you and defining who you are and what you need to do in order to truly know what you want and who you were meant to be.

We've reached the end of this journey. Your walk through the pages of this book is simply the beginning. You're now prepared to embark on your personal journey and find fulfillment. You will achieve critical success. You will inspire others. You will share your story, your 10-step book to critical success, and motivate someone close to you—your brother, your sister, your neighbor, maybe even your son or daughter. In this, most importantly, the sharing with others for the betterment of us all, you are an achiever of critical success.

Please do take the time to visit the following
Web site for more information:

WWW.2RULESOF3.COM

Go to WWW.THEHANDMILL.COM for
more interesting books by D.S. Brown

Coming in Spring 2008

An Educational Primer for the Majority Student

Knives, Forks, & Spoons

The CAP-GRAD Way!

Coming in Summer and Fall 2008

Media-Driven Consumercelebreality

3FE: Find, Focus, Establish the Fundamentals, Execute:
The Tool of Motivational Empowerment

An Educational Primer for the Majority Parent

Champion:
A Hero's Tale

When Love Is Not Enough

Anger and Thieves

When Atlanta Freaked

ABOUT THE AUTHOR

D.S. Brown is Derrick Sherroid Brown, a native of Atlanta, Georgia, and a true Southern Gentleman, with a passion for the written word. In the wee hours of the morning, you will find him making a concerted effort to delve into the world of his imagination. If not his imagination, then he will sift through facts to craft a worthy message to share with others. It is his sincerest desire that you find favor with what he writes. Enjoy his words. If you don't, then take a moment to tell him why.

Sirbrown@mindspring.com

Printed in the United States
103327LV00004B/223-318/P